CONVERSATIONS WITH MY RABBI

CONVERSATIONS *with* MY RABBI

Timeless Teachings for a Fractured World

RABBI ELI SCHLANGER AND
NIKKI GOLDSTEIN

HarperElement Spirit
An imprint of HarperCollins*Publishers*
1 London Bridge Street
London SE1 9GF

www.harpercollins.co.uk

HarperCollins*Publishers*
Macken House, 39/40 Mayor Street Upper
Dublin 1, D01 C9W8, Ireland

First published by HarperElement Spirit 2026

3 5 7 9 10 8 6 4 2

A catalogue record of this book is available from the British Library

ISBN 978-0-00-883336-7

Printed and bound in the UK using 100% renewable electricity at CPI Group (UK) Ltd

Designed by Bonni Leon-Berman

In loving memory of Rabbi Eli Schlanger,
from his devoted family

NIKKI: What's your mission?

RABBI ELI: To bring light. What's yours?

NIKKI: To bring love.

RABBI ELI: Excellent.

Male = Light (mind).

Female = Love (heart).

It's the perfect combination. Perfect Balance.

These things people call amazing coincidences, synchronicity, small miracles—this is the way life is supposed to be. Miracles should be normal.

As soon as you awaken to the purpose for which G-d sent you, this fractured, dreamy world shifts and its fragments merge into unison. Synchronized. Miraculous. As it was meant to be.

—*The Rebbe,*

Rabbi Menachem M. Schneerson

Contents

Preface

IN THE BEGINNING

This book is a conversation.

A real, raw, tender, sometimes funny, sometimes fierce exchange between a secular Jewish woman (me, Nikki) and a rabbi (him, Eli)—about what it means to live well, think deeply, and act ethically in a fractured world.

We had a shared goal. We wanted to offer something radically hopeful: a window into Jewish thought that is compassionate, relevant, and powerful. A body of work that would resonate across time and cultures. A way of seeing the world that has sustained a people through exile, trauma, miracles, and rebirth.

This book wasn't to be about preaching or converting anyone (it's not what we do as Jews anyhow) or proving anything. It was to be a vibrant, real-life dialogue between two people who genuinely wanted to make a difference.

The question-and-answer format of this book was drawn from our actual conversations. In *Conversations with My Rabbi*, we explored questions of faith, identity, morality, and purpose through the unique lens of Jewish wisdom. It was not to be academic, lofty, or out-of-reach knowledge, but worldly wisdom gained through lived experience and grounded by a framework of ancient teachings, the Noahide Laws. Simple, profound rules for living that have endured through time and continue to guide us in coexisting peacefully.

Though we wanted to light a flame in the hearts of Jews all over the world, this book was never meant to be *just* for Jews. It was to be for anyone looking for timeless inspiration in a chaotic world.

And then, on the evening of December 14, the unthinkable happened.

Rabbi Eli Schlanger (my rabbi) organised a Chanukah candle-lighting ceremony on Sydney's Bondi Beach. Bondi is home to Eli's Chabad synagogue and has been an idyllic haven for Jews since the early twentieth century. Jewish restaurants and social clubs sit alongside tattoo parlours, Italian pizza bars, and chic boutiques. It's a magnet for people from every corner of the globe, and it was Eli's backyard.

For eighteen years he'd organised "Chanukah by the Sea." It was the quintessential Eli event—families gathered, united in joy and prayer, for the festival of light. It was on brand and on mission for Eli, who would often say, "I want the whole world to light up with the Jewish flame."

Given today's climate of vicious antisemitism, he would have known there were some risks in being so identifiably Jewish in a public place—so much so, he had organised both police and additional security for the event. But when I once asked him if he was afraid of being an out and proud Jew, he simply said, "When they hate us, we don't hide, we don't cower, we become even more Jewish."

Witnesses report that around 6:41 p.m., two gunmen opened fire. Eli had just had his photo taken helping someone with their tefillin, and a minute or so later, he was dead.

That day, I'd been having lunch with friends. That prior engagement kept my husband, Rowan, and me from attending the ceremony at Bondi (and probably saved our lives). At 7:00 p.m. on the group chat for the lunch, we were in a text fest thanking the hosts when Katrina, one of the guests and a journalist, texted: "Gunshots at Bondi Beach. Lots of sirens and choppers en route."

Before I could process the words, my stomach sank, and I screamed downstairs to Rowan, "A shooting at Bondi . . . Eli."

We raced to turn on the television. Rowan, in his usual calm way, soothing me saying, "Surely not, don't jump to the worst conclusions, Eli will be okay," but I was already shaking, and tears were streaming down my face.

Moments later, Katrina texted again: "Nine dead apparently. Lighting of Menorah ceremony. Attack on Jewish community."

Without confirmation of the slain, I put on the group chat: "Oh God could be MY rabbi."

Only an hour before at lunch, I'd been telling my friends about *this* book and the joy of having Eli in my life. They were captivated.

By 8:00 p.m., I received a message from a friend from the Melbourne Jewish community. She sent a photo of Eli with the headline "Breaking News. Rabbi Eli Schlanger has been identified as one of the victims in the massacre at a Chanukah event at Bondi Beach in Sydney, Australia."

My husband and I fell into each other's arms. Rowan's body

trembled as he buried his head into my shoulder. Like a wounded animal, I wailed, my body collapsing under the weight of grief.

I didn't sleep much, but I woke up in the morning knowing that Eli's legacy, his mission to bring light and love to the world, would not die with him. Through the hours of conversations, he had prepared me to be his herald, his foot soldier, and his torch-bearer.

Today, Rowan and I attended Eli's funeral. The state premier of New South Wales, the Honourable Chris Minns, was there, as well as other politicians and a vast crowd of friends and family. Through a veil of tears and deep pain, Eli's father-in-law, Rabbi Yehoram Ulman, the chief rabbi who Eli assisted at the Bondi Chabad Centre, addressed the coffin and said in his eulogy, "Eli, from the moment you married Chaya you became a son to us as much as she's our daughter. And you became everything to me, my hands, my head, my heart, my feet . . . I relied on you for everything. You're my son, my friend, my confidant."

Rabbi Eli Schlanger was only forty-one years old when he was gunned down mercilessly, senselessly in a terror attack. In that shooting spree with high-powered weapons, two men killed fifteen people (at the time of writing) and injured at least forty others. Amongst the dead was a ten-year-old girl and an eighty-seven-year-old Holocaust survivor. Eli's two-month-old baby was injured in the attack, is currently in the hospital, and had a severe shrapnel wound to his leg. Chaya, Eli's wife, also had shrapnel wounds to her back.

This book was not supposed to happen like this. Eli was not

supposed to die before we'd finished. I still had one more chapter to discuss with him, ironically chapter 7, "What Does Justice Look Like?"

I feel immensely lucky to have met Rabbi Eli Schlanger. He left behind a beautiful young wife and five glorious children. Their baby will never know his father.

To me, Eli was a Jedi knight. His lightsaber was the love he radiated. Filling the world with joy was his raison d'être, it was his fuel and his compass. It's not that he was close to God, he was saturated and immersed in God. Eli found a place in himself where his light had merged with God, and anyone who met him felt it instantly. I did. Everyone did. And it was as magnetic as the sun pulling planets into its orbit.

Eli would hate me to dwell on sad things, in fact he would have only wanted me to focus on the light. So there is nothing further for me to say other than this book is for him, and it's designed to light the way for others.

May His Memory Be a Blessing.
Nikki Goldstein
December 17, 2025

Introduction

OUR SHARED STORY: THERE WAS LIGHT

On September 14, 2025, the phone rang. The name that popped up made me smile: Eli Schlanger.

We always seemed to be weirdly in sync, and the first thing I said was, "Funny you should call." Because just that morning, I'd been thinking about *this* book. *Our* book.

Eli was on his way to St. Vincent's Hospital—the very place where we'd met almost three years ago to the day.

I don't remember our first meeting.

I was in a coma.

ICU. Tubes everywhere. A machine was breathing for me. I'd been intubated just twenty-four hours earlier, barely clinging to life after pneumonia had overwhelmed my lungs. That morning, the head of the ICU had told my husband, Rowan, and my daughter, Liberty, to prepare for the worst.

While they sat at my bedside—watching, waiting, holding my hand—Liberty nudged Rowan and whispered, "Hey, Dad . . . is that a rabbi over there?"

Because I was unconscious, I heard this story much later, and this is their version, not mine.

Sure enough, there he was: a bearded, bespectacled man, not too tall, not too short, quick of step, firm of purpose, bright of eye, kippah in place, moving quickly through the queasy-making, overly lit ICU corridor. Rowan, not Jewish, bold and athletic, long of step, caught up with him in a few strides.

"Excuse me," Rowan said hesitantly. "Are you a rabbi?"

"Yes," Eli replied.

"My wife . . . she's in trouble. She might not make it. She's Jewish," Rowan said. "I think she'd want a prayer or blessing even though she doesn't go to synagogue . . . if you have the time."

Eli nodded. Grave. Present. And kind. He stepped quietly into the room, glanced at me—unmoving, unconscious, eyes closed—and turned to Rowan with a question: "What's her Jewish name?"

Rowan hesitated. Shrugged his shoulders. Looking lost for words. A little sheepishly, he admitted that neither he nor Liberty knew my Hebrew name.

Eli nodded, unfazed. "What about her mother's Hebrew name?"

Another pause. Another blank. More shrugged shoulders.

Still, Eli wasn't deterred. He asked, with warmth and gentleness, "Would it be all right if I blew the shofar?"

The shofar, he explained, is an ancient ram's horn, sounded on special days to stir the soul and open a pathway between this world and the Divine.

Rowan asked a nearby nurse, who looked a little surprised—this was, apparently, a first. Then, with a dry smile, she added, "As long as it's not too loud, it probably won't disturb anyone." She gestured toward the others in the ward. "Most of them," she said, "are comatose."

And so, right there in the ICU, Eli blew the shofar. They said its cry, amongst the sterile electronic "pinging" of machines, was deep and earthy. He spoke ancient prayers over my near-lifeless body. He offered comfort to my bewildered husband and terrified daughter. And then, he moved on.

Not that anything observable happened right then and there. I didn't miraculously awaken from my coma, but something shifted.

A day later, my lungs began to respond. The infection started to retreat. The medical team brought me out of the coma. I was thin, weak—but alive.

The doctors jokingly called it a miracle.

I did too.

Eli didn't "call" it a miracle.

He knew it was one.

When I was transferred to a general ward, I remember sitting up in bed, talking on the phone to one of my many doctors, when a Jewish man, clearly a rabbi, burst in with a bright smile and sparkling eyes.

"It's you!" he exclaimed. "You made it!"

It took me a moment. Then I realised: This must be *him*. My rabbi. The horn blower. The stranger-turned-soul-friend.

Eli explained that the shofar acts as a kind of cosmic reset. A channel clearer. A spiritual defibrillator.

His prayers, the prayers of my family and friends, excellent doctors, and my own stubborn will to live—somehow, they all found their mark.

Whatever the mark was, I came back.

That moment bonded us in a way that's hard to explain. Sacred. Unlikely. Eternal.

ELI'S TAKE ON OUR STORY: A SHOFAR IN THE ICU

It was the month of Elul—the final month in the Jewish calendar, a time of introspection, of returning, of soul-preparation before the High Holy Days. I had been called to the ICU to visit a man from our community who'd taken a sudden, serious turn.

I arrived with my tefillin in one hand and a shofar in the other. These are spiritual tools, yes—but also vessels of comfort, memory, and meaning. I stood quietly by the man's bedside, whispered prayers into the space between us, and sounded the shofar. A cry. A call. A trembling, ancient sound that reaches places words can't. Then, I left his room and continued on my way.

But just as I stepped into the corridor, a man approached me. He looked desperate and anxious.

"Rabbi," he said, "can you please come say a prayer with my wife? She's Jewish. I've had every religious minister in this hospital visit—but I haven't seen a rabbi until now."

I didn't hesitate. I followed him back into the ICU, where his wife lay unconscious. At her bedside sat their teenage daughter, head bowed, tears silently streaming down her face.

I explained the meaning of the shofar—that it's a spiritual wake-up call, a sound that pierces the heavens. It's not just heard—

it's *felt.* They both nodded. They understood more than words could explain. And so, I blew the shofar once more.

I said a prayer. I also shared the power of a simple act—giving charity, even a single coin each day. A small mitzvah, but one that carries great spiritual weight. They agreed to do it.

The moment passed. I left, not knowing what would come next.

A week later, I was back at the hospital for my regular rounds. I received my patient list, and there—unexpectedly—was Nikki's name.

But not in the ICU.

She was up on level nine. The recovery ward.

I rushed upstairs and walked onto her ward. She was sitting up in bed, on the phone with her doctor, looking strong. Her eyes caught mine as I entered. Kind, curious, calm—but also cautious.

"Please sit down, Rabbi," she said.

I waited while she finished her conversation. Then she looked at me again, more intently this time.

"I don't really know who you are," she said. "And I didn't understand much of what you did. But my husband and daughter told me everything. And what I do know is this—God has given me a second chance. I'm alive today because of the mitzvot [good deeds] you brought into that hospital room."

A month later, my daughter and I visited their home in northern Sydney. It was Sukkot—the Jewish festival of joy, gratitude, and impermanence. We stood together under the **sukkah** (a makeshift hut), shook the **lulav** (a palm frond) and **etrog** (a citron fruit), shared some sweet Kosher cakes, and raised a l'chaim.

There are moments in life that feel orchestrated from above. You can't plan them. You step into them—and try to show up fully.

This was one of those moments.

A shofar.

A prayer.

A coin.

A mitzvah.

A life.

A return.

SO, WHAT HAPPENED NEXT?

Since my big miracle, Eli and I became a part of each other's lives. We introduced each other to our families. We erased the lines between the secular and the religious. Between tradition and modernity. I joked that I was the only secular Jew he knew—then he gently corrected me, "There's no such thing as a secular Jew, we're just Jews."

We're different. And yet, at the core, we are the same.

We both want to do good. To serve. To uplift. Eli did it as a rabbi, ministering to his community with wisdom and warmth. I do it as a writer, telling stories, asking questions, chasing light.

This book was to be our shared offering. A way of sharing ancient teachings—some nearly six thousand years old—that still held the power to illuminate our modern lives.

This book was never meant to be just for Jews. It's for anyone seeking to live ethically, compassionately, spiritually—with integrity and truth.

We believed that sharing this wisdom was an act of courage—

and of hope. The Seven Noahide Laws, the backbone of this book, are a universal code of ethics offered by Judaism to the world.

I know that Rabbi Eli would feel as I do—that this story must be told. That these pages must be published and read by as wide an audience as possible. We once hoped that these pages would challenge you, inspire you, and invite you to open your own heart to the light. Now more than ever, we still do.

AN INTRODUCTION TO THE SEVEN NOAHIDE LAWS

A Universal Moral Code for an Age of Chaos

Before we dive into the heart of this book—into the big questions about faith, morality, purpose, and Jewish identity—we need to introduce the subtle thread that ties it all together: **The Seven Noahide Laws.**

These seven ancient laws are not as widely known as the Ten Commandments (until we started writing this book, I'd never heard of them), yet they contain within them a kind of spiritual DNA for all of humanity. They are not just *Jewish* laws—they are **universal**, meant for every person, everywhere.

And they are the moral compass guiding this book.

Where Do These Laws Come From?

The Noahide Laws—referring to Noah, the biblical figure who survived the great flood with his ark—are encoded and discussed within the **Babylonian Talmud** (Sanhedrin 56a). According to

Jewish tradition, after the flood wiped out a corrupt world, God gave Noah and his descendants seven foundational laws to build a just and compassionate civilisation.

These were not rituals or ethnic obligations. They weren't tied to a nation, tribe, or religion. They were—and still are—**a universal moral code.**

Later, when the Torah was given at Sinai, the Jewish people were charged with a more extensive covenant—613 commandments. But the Seven Noahide Laws, also outlined to Moses on Sinai, remained the **baseline ethical obligations for all people**, regardless of faith or background.

Even though part of the original commandment from God for the Noahide Laws was for Jews to share them with the world, they lay largely dormant for thousands of years because it wasn't safe for Jews to teach them. Then, in the twentieth century, Rabbi Menachem M. Schneerson (1902–1994), known universally as "the Rebbe," one of the most influential rabbis of modern times, reawakened knowledge of the Noahide Laws and sought to spread them globally.

What Are the Seven Noahide Laws?

DO NOT WORSHIP IDOLS.

Recognise and honour the One Creator. Do not elevate false gods, ideologies, or material pursuits above the Divine.

DO NOT BLASPHEME.

Respect the sanctity of the Divine. Use words with care. Do not blaspheme or treat the sacred with contempt.

DO NOT MURDER.
Preserve the sanctity of human life. Every life has infinite value and is sacred before God.

NO EATING FLESH FROM A LIVING ANIMAL.
Practice compassion toward animals. Avoid cruelty. Recognise that how we treat the vulnerable matters.

DO NOT STEAL.
Respect the property, dignity, and rights of others. Do not exploit, manipulate, or deceive.

DO NOT COMMIT ACTS OF SEXUAL IMMORALITY.
Protect the dignity of the body and the sacredness of relationships. The family unit is the foundation of human society. Honour the moral boundaries of intimacy.

ESTABLISH COURTS OF JUSTICE.
Create systems of fairness and accountability. Pursue justice. Uplift society. Every small act of justice restores harmony to our world.

Why These Laws Matter Today

Rabbi Eli was passionate about the Noahide Laws because he saw them as an enduring symbol of civility, morality, ethics, and connection to God. It was also part of his mission as handed down by his spiritual teacher, the Rebbe. He fervently believed they offered a way to restore order and balance to a chaotic world. As modern humans, overwhelmed by division, noise, and moral relativism, the Noahide Laws offer something rare: **clarity**.

They are **not political**. They are **not dogmatic**.

They are **deeply ethical**, rooted in the idea that **human beings are co-creators of a just world.**

You don't need to be Jewish to find meaning in them. In fact, these laws are specifically *not* Jewish in the ethnic or ritual sense. They are **spiritual scaffolding for all of us**—a way to bring more truth, compassion, and integrity into our lives, homes, and communities.

They remind us that:

- Life is sacred.
- Justice is not optional.
- Words matter.
- Compassion is holy.
- There is One Source behind it all.

They don't require religious belief—but they ask us to live as if our actions matter. Because they do.

Why We Chose These Laws as the Framework for This Book

We chose the Noahide Laws because they give us a structure that is:

- **Ancient**, yet completely **relevant**.
- **Grounded**, yet open to deep spiritual exploration.
- **Universal**, yet rich with Jewish insight.

Each chapter in this book loosely corresponds to one of these seven laws, not as a strict rulebook, but as a starting point and **framework for conversation.**

Because Judaism is a tradition of questions, of dialogue, of wrestling with ethics, morals, and the Divine, these seven laws provide the moral clarity needed to have those conversations with humility and courage.

There's no right way to read this book. You can start anywhere. You can underline things, skip things, and argue with things. That's all Kosher.

The Noahide Laws remind us that God doesn't expect us to be perfect.

God wants us to **be engaged.**

WHY WE'RE HAVING THIS CONVERSATION

NIKKI: Eli, can I be honest? I almost didn't write this book.

RABBI ELI: That's the best place to start. Total honesty. Go on.

NIKKI: Because I thought—who am I to ask these questions? I'm not religious. I never light Shabbat candles on Fridays. I believe fervently in God, but I consider myself spiritual (not in a fluffy way, but in a deep way), not observant. I've studied philosophy, meditation, and Ayurvedic healing. But Torah? Talmud? Hebrew? I feel like a tourist in my own tradition.

RABBI ELI: You're not alone. A lot of people feel that way. Especially Jews who weren't raised observant, or who left it behind. But that discomfort is an invitation, not a disqualification.

NIKKI: I guess I just wanted to know: Do Judaism and the Noahide code, that we're about to discuss, still have anything to say to people like me—secular, modern, spiritual-but-not-always-practising—especially in a world that is so full of distractions and demands?

RABBI ELI: Judaism has everything to say! To the seekers, the sceptics, the cultural Jews, the allies, the wounded, the world-weary. Our tradition was built for long journeys and uncomfortable questions.

NIKKI: So, this book is me showing up with all my questions—and you answering with profound, sometimes surprising Jewish wisdom.

RABBI ELI: And sometimes with more questions. That's the Jewish way.

CHAPTER 1

Tell Me Why I Should Believe in God?

NOAHIDE LAW 1: DO NOT WORSHIP IDOLS

(Know God)

Make a joyful shout to the Lord, all you lands . . . Know that the Lord, He is God; It is He who has made us, and . . . We are His.

PSALMS 100:1–3

ꟹ

THE ORIGINS OF THE FIRST LAW: DO NOT WORSHIP IDOLS

The first of the Seven Noahide Laws stands as one of the cornerstones of Western moral and spiritual life. It begins not with commandments, but with a relationship: One God, one world, and one human family.

In a time when the noise of the media is deafening, trust in our institutions is crumbling, and our world feels dangerously fractured, this law offers something rare: a steady place to stand. It calls on us to discover how to be our best selves, to set aside our differences, and to explore—perhaps for the very first time—what it truly means to believe in God. Not God as an abstract concept, but God as a living, Divine presence greater than ourselves.

This first law rests on a profound premise: There is one God, one Source, and it underpins everything—the physical world, the human world, the spiritual world. To the ancients, one God represented a revolutionary break from polytheism that changed every aspect of life. To the modern Western mind, it whispers something equally bold: *Don't be dazzled by the surface. Reject the mirages and false gods of our age.* This law invites us to see through the illusions and to embrace the unseen—but very real—presence of God. A leap of faith? Perhaps. But it is the vital, life-giving first step toward building something new.

The invitation to believe in God, and the prohibition against idolatry, find their roots in Genesis and are made explicit in the Ten Commandments:

I am the Lord your God . . .
You shall have no other gods before Me.
You shall not make for yourself . . . You shall
not bow down to them or serve them.

—Exodus 20:2–5

The ancient world overflowed with idols. People worshipped the sun, the moon, fertility goddesses, kings, and carved stone. Entire systems of belief elevated power, nature, and even human rulers into divine figures. Animals—and sometimes humans—were sacrificed to appease angry, hungry, or jealous gods.

Into this chaos came Abraham.

Abraham is celebrated as the first monotheist—not because he received a Divine commandment, but because he dared to search. He looked at the stars, the sun, the world around him, and despite their popular appeal and empty promises, he said quietly but firmly: *"This can't be all there is."* He smashed his father's idols and broke with everything his culture held sacred.

And here is where something remarkable happened. A new possibility entered the frame, and humanity found itself with a choice: Instead of appeasing a volatile pantheon of jealous, competing gods, we were offered something far more beautiful—a single relationship to tend. A relationship of love and Divine connection. Intimacy with the Source. One God. Not a being to be placated with offerings, but a Creator to be known and to be known by.

> For thus says the Lord, Who created the heavens, Who is God, Who formed the earth and made it, Who has established it, Who did not create it in vain, Who formed it to be inhabited.
>
> —Isaiah 45:18

So, what happened next? God gave humanity the means to formalise this relationship—the tools to build a just and civil society—the Noahide Laws. As Rabbi Eli explains, these laws matter deeply: "It's only through a set of rules and guardrails that humans can do what they're meant to do here on earth—fulfil their Godly potential and realise God's plan, which is ultimately to be in a relationship with Him."

And the law against idolatry, he says, is foundational to that relationship. "It stands to reason we can't be connected to the one God if we're worshipping at many altars." God invites constancy and devotion—not distraction and infidelity.

This law is not simply "Don't bow down to statues." It is something far richer: *Don't trade truth for illusion. Don't give your heart to things unworthy of it.*

These days, Rabbi Eli reminds us, we're not bowing before golden calves—but we still worship plenty of false gods. "In the modern world," he says, "we idolise fame, beauty, money, youth, power. We worship ourselves on Instagram. We chase Likes like they're eternal."

To "not worship idols" in the twenty-first century is to reject those false altars. It is to refuse to elevate the temporary above the eternal. It is to remember that while the world dazzles and distracts momentarily, only the Divine endures.

And there is something even deeper here, something that anchors us morally and spiritually as humans and elevates us beyond the transient and temporal. . . . If we are made in the image of God, and there is only one God, then every human being carries a reflection of that holiness. That belief becomes the beating heart beneath all other ethical laws.

This first law among the seven is not simply a religious rule. It is a radical declaration of unity: one God, one truth, one shared humanity. And on that foundation—solid, ancient, and still quietly revolutionary—we can begin to build a just and civil society that enfolds and embraces all of us.

Welcome to a new world.

A NOTE ON OUR CONVERSATION

We all saw it coming. Australia recorded 1,654 anti-Jewish incidents in 2025. And it's not only here in Australia, it's clear that there is now a global antisemitism emergency. The cost of politicians, universities, institutions, and the media turning a blind eye was my friend's death.

Eli and I talked a lot about antisemitism and how to deal with it. I would say things like, "How can there be a God when such acts of hate are perpetrated against us?" And he always came back with a simple answer: "When they hate us, we become more Jewish. Do you know why? Because God dwells within each human being, and when we show His light, through our actions and deeds, we elevate the world and that love and light quells the hate."

In the wake of his death—only a few days ago as I write this—I am struggling with my faith. I'm finding it hard to reconcile with a God who allows this to happen. I wish Eli were here to do what he did, shine light and inspire me with his unshakable faith.

At the outset of this project, Eli said, "I don't want this book to be negative. I want it to inspire and illuminate the world." I agreed, but being Jewish at this time in history is perilous. We have to balance what's happening in the world with what's happening in our hearts. What I know Eli would want is for his words to provide comfort and solace in the aftermath of all this destruction.

I was told by someone who was at the shooting, that before they could light the first candle of the menorah at "Chanukah by the Sea," the event Eli had organised for eighteen years at Bondi Beach, he became aware of the gunman, and while everyone hit the ground, Eli stood, raised his arms, and tried to negotiate with the gunman—looking for another way. . . . To the end, he was protecting his community. He radiated joy from every fibre of his being. As I'm trying to come to terms with his loss, which makes me question God, I am reminded that God shows his face on earth in a myriad of ways—sometimes tragic and terrible and sometimes beautiful and miraculous, but always mysterious and enigmatic.

Eli trying to bring love and light to a man whose gun is aimed at him, a gun that ends his life, is an image that will endure forever in my mind. What does it mean? A snapshot in time when joy turns to sorrow and reveals God's ineffable power. Eli would have told me, with his impish smile, that even though we can't see God's plan, He nevertheless has one.

This chapter is about eschewing false idols and trusting that there's a single Divine Source. Eli and I experienced God differently, but at the end of the day, we both believed that our God is a god of love, peace, light, communion, and connection

It feels more important than ever that we find ways to live together in civil, safe, and loving ways.

The Noahide Laws do just that.

NIKKI: Let's get right to the heart of the matter. Maybe an obvious question, but we Jews ask a lot of questions. Right? Most people don't get to ask a rabbi questions, but I'm sitting here in front of mine, so I'm going to ask the unaskable.

Why do you believe in God?

RABBI ELI: Every part of me "knows" God is God. God is not abstract. God is real. God is within every single atom and creature in the universe. Everything that exists has the constant power of God giving it life. God is the very essence of this world. And not just this world—every world, every being, every moment.

NIKKI: But how do you connect with something that can't be seen, touched, or proven?

RABBI ELI: Not everything real is visible. Look at wi-fi. Bluetooth. Electricity. You can't see them. But they're everywhere. We just assume the machines will work—powered by some invisible something. The same is true with God. You don't have to see Him to know He's there.

NIKKI: Eli, tell me more. Your faith really inspires me, but if I can't see or more importantly *feel* God, then why should I believe in Him?

RABBI ELI: I've been at the bedside of people who are dying, it's how you and I met, and I've been to prisons and seen people in a lot of pain, and I believe that most people have a deep knowing that God isn't far away. It might not be a conscious thought, but there's a seed of that Divine spark inside everyone, and often in extreme joy or extreme pain people really *feel* it—as you say.

NIKKI: So how do you define God?

RABBI ELI: (He smiles) How do you define something infinite? I'll tell you, he's not sitting in the sky on a throne with a long flowing white beard. He's within every single thing that exists. Certainly, not just within Jews! Not just within humans. Within animals. Trees. Rocks. Time. God is the constant force behind every form of life. If that force stopped for even a second, the universe wouldn't just die—it would vanish. It wouldn't exist. God was, God is, and God always will be. He's not limited to anything.

NIKKI: If God is *everywhere* in the universe, why can't we see Him?

RABBI ELI: We're playing hide-and-seek. God hides—not to punish us; on the contrary, He hides to give us the joy of discovery.

Like a parent hiding behind a tree so their child can find them and squeal with delight. That moment of reunion is powerful. That's what God wants—not robotic belief, but eager, willing connection.

The world we see with our "eyes of flesh"—as our sages say—isn't the ultimate reality. The physical world is not the whole story. What's invisible is often more real than what's visible.

Kabbalah teaches, and this is explained at great length in Chabad Chassidism, the tradition that shaped my worldview, that before the world was created, there was only God. Total oneness. No time, no space. Just Infinite Light.

To allow creation, God had to *contract* that light. That contraction is called *Tzimtzum*. It's like turning down the voltage so that the Divine energy won't overwhelm the system. Just like a phone charger has to regulate electricity so your phone doesn't explode—God "transformed" His light so the world could exist.

NIKKI: That's stunning. It leaves me breathless.

RABBI ELI: And this is the miracle of existence—that we're living in a perfectly measured balance between the hidden and the revealed.

That's why the sages say the world is like a marriage: spirit and matter, soul and body. It's our job to unite them. And most often we spend a lifetime doing so, for the benefit of God Himself, the world around us, our families and ourselves.

NIKKI: This is something many people, both outside and inside of Judaism, struggle with, and it often gets us into trouble. Do you think Jews have a special place in God's universe?

RABBI ELI: We believe that every single human being has been handpicked and chosen by God for a specific purpose and mission in this world—a holy mission. We absolutely do not believe you have to be Jewish to be close to God, or to have a relationship with God. But we do believe there's a reason for everything God does—where God puts each of us in this world and why he's put us in that time and that place. It's also important to understand that whether you're Jewish or not, we believe there is an obligation for every human to elevate the world and the people around you—not from a place of superiority (we don't believe we're superior at all!), but because that's why we're here on earth, to fulfil God's mission.

NIKKI: Not everyone has this feeling. What do you say to people who don't have this inner knowing or this direct connection to God?

RABBI ELI: It's a bit like an arranged marriage. The love doesn't come at first, it takes time and it often happens when you do little things for the other person. Trust and love build when you show up. This is what God wants—showing up. Doing the practices, gifts of service build the relationship. Prayer, contemplation, being conscious every day of the mitzvot (kind deeds) you do for others, and to willingly and generously serve God. They all add up.

NIKKI: But what if someone doesn't believe? Can you call yourself a Jew and not believe in God? I always believed in God, but it's only recently, and maybe because of my near-death experience, that I now identify with the God of my ancestors. What about people who feel culturally or ethnically Jewish, but don't necessarily believe in God?

RABBI ELI: Every Jew, and every human being, believes in God—even if they say they don't. I'll tell you why. Imagine someone says, "I don't believe in God." I'll tell them: "If you truly didn't believe, why are you so interested in abandoning Him?" You can't already be in a relationship with something you don't think exists.

It's like the story of the father who tells his child:

"There is only one God in the world—and we don't believe in Him."

Even in denial, God is present.

NIKKI: So then, let's get to the idolatry aspect of this Law: Why do we still have the "no idolatry" rule? What does that mean in today's world? We're not exactly building golden calves anymore.

RABBI ELI: The ancient idea of bowing to a statue is mostly gone. But the notion of idolatry is alive and well—just in more subtle forms. Celebrity worship, materialism, ego, power, self-deification—these are our modern idols. Anything that replaces our awareness of God, anything that takes over our sense of purpose and wonder, becomes an idol.

NIKKI: So really, this law is about seeing past illusion. It's about spiritual clarity and belief. That's very counterintuitive for a lot of people. Today's world says, "I'll believe it when I see it."

RABBI ELI: But in Judaism, it's the opposite: *You'll see it when you believe it.* Kabbalah teaches that what we call "nothingness"—the unseen—is actually the deepest "something." It's called *Ayin*, which literally means "nothing," but it refers to the Source of everything.

Many things in Judaism are both counterintuitive and have a reversed meaning.

I'm going to need a minute to tell you a story to explain an interesting principle of Jewish thinking, teaching, and discussion called *leshon sagi nahor*. It's the concept of inverted or euphemistic reversed meanings and it's going to come up a bit more in our discussions, so I may as well explain it here.

In Aramaic, *sagi nahor* literally means "a lot of light" or "great light." But here's the twist: In the Talmud, it's actually used to refer to someone who is blind.

NIKKI: Wait—so they call a blind person "full of light"? That sounds like an early form of Jewish humour.

RABBI ELI: It's actually an example of gentle, euphemistic language. Rabbi Sheshet was one of the leading sages from the early to mid-fourth century CE, whose teachings appear throughout the Babylonian Talmud: He was physically blind, but we all know there are two ways of "seeing"—through our physical eyes and through our spiritual eyes, and he was a great seer in the mystical sense. That's why the Talmud refers to him as "abundant in light." It's ironic on the surface, but the idea is not only to avoid speaking harshly or shamefully about a disability, but also to understand the deeper meaning, that we don't see only with our eyes.

NIKKI: That's kind of beautiful . . . and also a little ironic.

RABBI ELI: Exactly. A *sagi nahor* may lack the eyes to see the physical world but has an abundance of inner or spiritual light.

NIKKI: So, Judaism has this way of using language that masks or inverts the true meaning of things?

RABBI ELI: Yes. And quite often when the Bible or the Sages want to talk about something challenging or upsetting, the language is flipped rather than saying it bluntly.

Take Job's wife, for example. She tells him, literally: "Bless God and die" (Job 2:9). The actual meaning in context is really "*Blaspheme* God and die." Here, some Bible translations use the opposite word, "bless," as a kind of verbal shield.

NIKKI: So, it's like holy sarcasm?

RABBI ELI: You could say "holy euphemism." Much later—in the nineteenth century—this kind of ironic, obscured language, *leshon sagi nahor* ("the language/idiom of *sagi nahor*") was employed even in regular daily speaking.

NIKKI: So, the phrase travelled from a Talmudic description for someone with a visual impairment to a modern term for saying the opposite of what you intend, to soften or disguise something?

RABBI ELI: Exactly. And unless you know the backstory, that *sagi nahor* began as this Talmudic phrase about a blind sage, you'd never guess it from the literal words "great light."

NIKKI: Even this one little expression is like an archaeological dig into Jewish history and language. Fascinating!

RABBI ELI: Yes. It shows how a phrase, or an approach, can carry layers of history and meaning: from the Bible to the Talmud, through medieval Kabbalah, and into the modern usage in Yiddish and Hebrew speech and literature.

NIKKI: I love that—this tiny phrase opening a whole world. But how does any of this "careful language" connect to idolatry?

RABBI ELI: Beautiful question. Because on the surface they seem like totally different topics: Blind rabbis, euphemisms . . . and bowing down to statues.

NIKKI: Right. One sounds like a linguistics seminar, and the other sounds like a scene from *The Ten Commandments*.

RABBI ELI: But there is a deep link: Both idolatry and *lashon hakodesh*—the holy language (Hebrew)—are about what we do with our imagination. How we construct our inner worlds, the architecture of which is language, forms the basis of our actions and ethics. Do we let words and images point to something higher, or do we freeze them and worship them?

NIKKI: If I understand you correctly, you're saying idolatry is like turning a metaphor into a god?

RABBI ELI: Totally! God knows we often attribute meaning to things that don't deserve our reverence. The mind lands on the "thing" and says **this is it**! But that's not the whole picture. God is "behind" the scene—and that's what **this law is directing us to do, to look beyond.**

NIKKI: It's like confusing the signpost for the destination.

RABBI ELI: If you keep saying, "This power, this thing, this idea is everything, this is my ultimate," you're literally worshipping it. It starts in the imagination and the mind and words form to support the idea, then it takes shape at the lips, and once it's out of your mouth, it becomes a real thing. The First Noahide Law steps in and says, "Stop. Don't give ultimate status to a false god. Don't give your heart away to something illusory and temporary and forget the Source."

NIKKI: In modern terms, that sounds less like bowing to a golden calf and more like worshipping money, fame, and success. We don't carve statues; we download apps.

RABBI ELI: The external form always changes. The inner dynamic is the same. Idolatry happens when something finite takes the throne in your inner world. And then we justify it: *"I'm doing it for my family"* or *"Everyone's doing it."*

NIKKI: I guess in the parlance of our contemporary spiritual *leshon sagi nahor* we'd call it "doing the work" or "self-actualisation," but really, it's "I will sacrifice everything to this one thing and call it modern living." But strip away the pretty words and self-delusion and it's worshipping at a false altar and sacrificing my values to a false god.

RABBI ELI: Right. We use clever language to avoid admitting the ugly truth: "I'm giving my soul away." That's why the First Noahide Law isn't only about high-level theology. It's also about devotion. Who gets your deepest "yes"? Who gets your ultimate trust?

We're often not even conscious that we're worshipping a false god, but we're sure not connecting to the Divine when we're shouting down the phone at someone, driving too fast to too many appointments, and stressing over bills or the kids' homework.

NIKKI: And given we've been talking about words and language, where does God's name fit into this? Because Jews won't even say the Name. We say *Hashem* ("The Name") instead. Is that another form of holy euphemism?

RABBI ELI: It is, and it's deeply connected to not worshipping idols. Jewish law tells us not to pronounce the four-letter Name of God—the Tetragrammaton, written in Hebrew as a *Yod*, a *Hei*, and a *Vav*, and then another *Hei*—because it represents "I am who I am" or

"He causes to be" and is considered too holy to utter. Instead, we say *Hashem*—"The Name"—in conversation (and in prayer we use some of His other names). On one level, yes, it's a euphemism. On a deeper level, it's saying: "Any name I address You with is only partial. I will not pretend I have captured You in a syllable."

NIKKI: So not saying the Name is itself an anti-idolatry move. It's like: "I won't shrink You down to something I can easily label."

RABBI ELI: Idolatry says, "I want a god I can see, measure, control." The First Noahide Law says, "No. Connect to the One you can't reduce down to anything the human mind can consume, control, or contain." And in our careful day-to-day language, *Hashem* is a way of keeping that humility alive. Unless you're Moses on Mount Sinai, you don't get to talk as if you see the whole picture.

NIKKI: So, when we talk about *Ayin*—that sacred nothingness—and now *sagi nahor* and these holy euphemisms, you're really building a kind of linguistic and conceptual fence around the first law.

RABBI ELI: I haven't thought about it like that, but yes, let's call it a fence made of humility. Judaism is **obsessed** with how we speak, because speech is where the inner and outer worlds meet. If I train myself to speak lightly of God, or to speak as if money or power are absolute, my inner map rearranges itself accordingly. Soon, I won't just talk like an idolator. I *feel* like one, and I am one.

NIKKI: And then I sacrifice my kids to my career, my body to my addictions, my integrity to the crowd.

RABBI ELI: That's right. And the tragedy is, no one thinks "I'm worshipping an idol." We say, "I'm just doing what everyone does." That's why these "simple" Noahide Laws are actually so radical: They say to every human being, "You are capable of so much more than just the default setting of your culture. You can refuse to bow down to a false god—even if the whole world is bowing down to a false god."

HOW TO RESIST THE SEDUCTION OF MODERN IDOLS

NIKKI: So how does an ordinary person, scrolling Instagram, drinking their lattes, actually *practice* the first law?

RABBI ELI: A straightforward place to begin is to become mindful of all God gives us. It's pretty easy to take a moment to breathe and thank God for the beauty of creation. You don't have to be a religious person to do this, it's just a pause in our busy lives. If you want to go further, become conscious of how you say God's name. Pause before you say, "Oh God," especially when you're frustrated at work or queueing at the supermarket. Think of these as pattern interruptions: Here are a few simple tweaks that pack a big punch.

Invite Goodness into Your Life with Gratitude

- **PAUSE AND THINK**
  "I didn't create my own life, and I'm not in full control of outcomes." Even when you're busy or especially when you're stressed, this subtle reframe helps you acknowledge something beyond yourself—providence, grace, luck, support, life itself—God. Suddenly you're off the hook for the outcome, it's let go and let God—a simple and effective way to allow God to enter the space.
- **RINSE AND REPEAT**
  Throughout the day, whenever something good happens, say, *"Thank God."* Or, *"Blessed be God!"* You may have heard Jewish people saying this last statement in Hebrew, *"Baruch Hashem."* In fact, it's flexible—say *"Baruch Hashem"* with a smile when life is sweet, or whisper it humbly when life is heavy. It's a subtle and gentle way of keeping your footing in an uncertain world.

Gratitude and blessing bring instant humility and instant joy. It's better than any drug. Everything else—every idol, every image, every obsession—is just a passing shadow in that great light.

AND WHAT ABOUT TAMING THE BEAST OF DESIRE?

NIKKI: We've talked about idols and language and *what* we worship. But what about the raw stuff—desire itself? Our actual human cravings for food, sex, attention, and success. The commandment doesn't tell us to become monks. So . . . what do we *do* with all of that?

RABBI ELI: The problem isn't that we're walking bundles of desire. The problem is what throne we put those desires on.

Let's start with the basics. In classic Jewish language, you have the **yetzer tov** and the **yetzer hara**—the pull toward goodness and the pull toward self-gratification. The Torah hints at this in Genesis when it says, "the inclination of the human heart is evil from youth," which the rabbis understand as the ego and self-focused drive that shows up very early in life.

Hasidic philosophy zooms in even more. It talks about the **human soul** (*nefesh ha'chiyunit*), which contains the Divine spark, and the **animal soul** (*Nefesh HaBehemit*). The animal soul isn't necessarily "evil"—it's more like an untrained toddler. It just wants comfort, pleasure, security. It's the part of us that craves the extra glass of wine, the late-night scroll, the hit of validation. And if left to its own devices can devolve into some messy stuff. Urging us in the other direction, the Divine spark within us longs for meaning, transcendence, love, and a Divine connection to God. Healthy spiritual life is about encouraging the animal soul to work for the Divine one. And this takes practice and discipline.

NIKKI: If I understand correctly, you're saying that Judaism doesn't ask us to "kill our desire," it's telling us to "house-train it."

RABBI ELI: Or in Hasidic language: **Don't crush the animal—harness its energy in the service of good.**

To get a bit technical and go a bit deeper here, the Tanya (the foundational text of Chabad Chassidism, by Rabbi Schneur Zalman of Liadi, also known as the Alter Rebbe, which serves as the master spiritual guidebook for navigating the epic struggle between the competing Divine and animal soul powers inside each human being), goes further to say, the animal soul can at times even be *trained* to **crave spiritual pleasure more** than physical pleasure through performing mitzvot and studying God's wisdom. It's a way of teaching your inner toddler that there are higher forms of play.

NIKKI: Okay, that's the theory. What are the *actual practices* that help with that? Because I suspect that our desires do not respond to theory.

RABBI ELI: Well, this is where the other five Noahide principles will soon come into play. The first two anchor all the other Noahide Laws in their belief and accountability to God. Then the others give us guardrails to prevent us sinking towards our worst human instincts—and a framework to live our best lives in harmony with our fellow humans and tread softly on the earth.

Training Desire at the Table

NIKKI: Okay you've got me wanting more of the good stuff now.

RABBI ELI: Let's start at the most basic level: **eating**. Torah doesn't say, "Food is dangerous, avoid it." Instead, it says, "Bless. Slow down. Restrict a bit. Eat with awareness." Choosing what you eat—and how you eat—with awareness, when to stop, how much wine you pour—those micro-acts of self-restraint or consciousness around food help prevent desire from running the show and turning into worship.

We'll talk more about this when we discuss the Fourth Noahide Law, *Do not eat the flesh of a living animal*, but from a mystical perspective, every piece of food holds a **spark of Divine energy**. When you eat mindlessly, you just feed your animal soul. When you make a blessing and hold the intention to use the energy you get from food to do good in the world and serve God, you feed the sacred spark inside you too. That's Kabbalah's project of **elevating sparks**—*birur hanitzotzot*.

NIKKI: So every "Baruch atah . . ." before coffee is a tiny anti-idolatry ritual?

RABBI ELI: What you're saying is: "This cup is not God. The caffeine is not God. It's a gift, a channel." That sentence already shifts your desire by one click—from "I need this" to "I'm *receiving* this from God and I am grateful to Him."

Daily Prayer and Hitbonenut: Brain Above Heart

NIKKI: What about when my desires feel like a storm in my chest? Is there a daily spiritual "gym" to keep them in check?

RABBI ELI: Yes—**tefillah** (prayer) and **hitbonenut** (meditative reflection). The Tanya has this very striking teaching: It says our animal drive lives primarily in the **heart**, while our Divine spark is rooted mainly in the **mind**, and that the natural order of a human is that "the brain rules the heart."

Prayer is when you give your Divine soul the microphone. You focus your mind on certain truths—God's oneness, gratitude, compassion—allow those thoughts to percolate through and positively affect the emotions.

And then you turn to face heaven and pray out loud (or whisper) to God. It's not about reciting special Hebrew; it's about rewiring your inner hierarchy by addressing God in a language that comfortably expresses your earnest connection to the Divine.

NIKKI: So instead of autopilot-reacting to whatever I feel first and caving in to my desires, I pause to give my higher mind a chance to speak?

RABBI ELI: Kabbalistically, this is the work of **tefillah** and **hitbonenut**. It's when an idea stops being abstract information and starts being your inner reality, your inner compass. Desire is powerful; you can't just shout at it. You have to **educate and redirect** it—through contemplation, through words, through willpower and routine.

Shabbat: Stepping Off the Hamster Wheel

NIKKI: What about the big weekly thing—Shabbat? Because that feels like a ritual break on the wheel of desire.

RABBI ELI: Shabbat is at the centre of Jewish spiritual mojo. For six days, we run after the world. On the seventh day, we stop and let the world run *without* us.

Kabbalistically, Shabbat isn't just a day off. It's described as a state of **Divine harmony**, where the inner structure of God's relationship with the world "rests"—a cosmic realignment that we plug into once a week.

NIKKI: That's a very poetic way of saying "log off your email" and "stop doomscrolling."

RABBI ELI: And it's accurate. On Shabbat, you deliberately **refuse to serve** your usual idols: busy-ness, money, the phone, the inbox. You're not allowed to "create" in the weekday technical sense, so you discover a deeper form of creativity—relationship, prayer, song, rest—a chance to reset not just your body and spirit, but to recharge your connection to God. Practically, Shabbat says to your desires: "You are not running the show—faith is, love is, peace is, rest is."

Which is why such a big chunk of the Shabbat liturgy is about **delight**—*oneg Shabbat*—good food, song, intimacy. The goal isn't to erase pleasure. The goal is to **sanctify** it by returning it to its Source.

While chunks of the Shabbat laws were commanded specifically to the Jewish people (to fulfil many of their additional commandments), there are so many takeaways for all modern people. Who wouldn't benefit from unplugging the phone, dialing down the busy-ness quotient, spending more time with friends and family? And if we take a leaf out of the Shabbat playbook, we could spend time reading Torah, reflecting on the week that has passed, and making resolutions for how to improve the world in the week to come.

Tzedakah and Chesed—The Practice of Giving

NIKKI: Okay, food, Shabbat, prayer. What about the desire to *take*, to get more for me? That's a false idol if ever I saw one. "Me, me, me" is virtually the mantra of our culture, and we worship the self and the individual as though they are the supreme goals of life.

RABBI ELI: That's where **tzedakah** (giving) and **chesed** (kindness) come in. The Rebbe taught that the single most important mitzvah for our generation is tzedakah. He believed that to nurture the personality of a **"giver"** was one of the most noble ways to demonstrate God's gift to the world.

The Kabbalah describes God's flow to the world as **Chesed**—expansive generosity. When you give, especially when you don't "feel like it," you are literally **aligning your inner wiring** with that Divine flow. Giving is the opposite of taking and unplugs us from the narcissistic aspect of Western culture.

On a psychological level, giving from a sacred and holy mindset breaks the story that all my energy must go toward my own accumulation—money, attention, power. On a mystical level, it says: "My desire to **have** is now serving my desire to **give**." The same drive that wanted to buy a third pair of shoes is now being retrained to enjoy feeding another person's dignity. It's something we teach our children every day.

And to extract the spiritual juice out of that—it starts with acknowledging and understanding that we were all created by God for a higher purpose than just feeding our desires and worshipping the false idols that society dangles before us.

NIKKI: So, to take it back a notch, is this right: I'm not supposed to hate my need for pleasure; I'm supposed to expand what counts as pleasurable?

RABBI ELI: The Kabbalists say the real spiritual work isn't to stop desiring, which is impossible, but instead, as soon as we become conscious of an inappropriate desire, to divert our attention onto something else—not in a distracted way, but in order to shake its hold over us. Another tool is to **expand our desire until God fits inside it.** There's even a line of teaching that asks: "Why do you want what you want? For what purpose?" If the intention becomes to serve something higher, the desire itself gets Divine backing.

Honest Self-Accounting and Curious Mindfulness

NIKKI: And what if you're just . . . failing at all of this?

RABBI ELI: Then you're in excellent company. That's where **cheshbon hanefesh**—"soul-accounting"—comes in. Commentaries like the *Chovos Halevavos* (Duties of the Heart) map out a ladder of traits—**awareness/consciousness, alacrity, purity, holiness**—and ask you to check in honestly: "Where did my desires run the show today? Where did I channel them?"

It's not about self-loathing, it's about **intentional self-honesty.**

Being mindful: "I notice that when I'm tired, I scroll for an hour. When I feel rejected, I go online shopping. Okay. How can I build one tiny practice that directs that same energy to somewhere holier?"

NIKKI: The answer to desire isn't simply "quash your desire," it's "know your desire"?

RABBI ELI: Beautifully put. Know it, and then, little by little, feed it experiences of goodness and holiness, until it develops some muscle memory. You might even discover that in time the heat of your desires cools and you start craving more of the good stuff without any prompting or practice. But be on your guard, your desires can hit you from behind when you least expect them.

NIKKI: If I zoom out, the First Noahide Law tells me not to worship idols—but instead to worship one God. And all these practices—blessings, Shabbat, prayer, giving, self-reflection—are practical tools for not turning my desires *into* idols and helping to connect me with God.

RABBI ELI: Yes! One hundred percent! Every time you bless before you eat, you're saying: "This food is not god, it was given to me *by* God."

Every Shabbat you keep, you're saying: "My work is not God."

Every time you give tzedakah, you're saying: "My money is not God."

Every honest conversation you have with your own heart, you're saying: "Even my desires are not God."

And Kabbalah adds that **underneath those desires lies the spark of Godliness.** Your goal is not to crush it, but to elevate it.

TELL US MORE ABOUT KABBALAH?

NIKKI: You've mentioned Kabbalah a lot today in the context of this First Noahide Law. How does it fit in with what we're talking about?

RABBI ELI: Kabbalah is the soul of the Torah. It's the inner code. It teaches the secrets and hidden workings of the world, starting with Creation itself, and provides insight into the mysteries of how we operate.

The danger is when people jump into the spiritual fire without grounding. It's like taking a heavy drug without medical supervision. That's why Kabbalah was traditionally kept hidden. Not because it was elitist—but because it was powerful.

We're lucky we have revered teachers like the Rebbe to show us the way. He, and the six Chabad Rebbes who preceded him, revealed secrets that previous generations didn't know—but delivered in a way that can be more readily understood and applied to modern daily life.

NIKKI: What about people who find faith through pain? Is that valid? That's probably what happened to me.

RABBI ELI: Very. There are two accelerated ways people find God: through joy or through struggle. Of course, in an ideal world it would be great if everyone came to God through love and gratitude. But when someone reaches for God in heartbreak—when they've lost something or feel alone—that moment is holy. It's like a child running to their parent after falling off their bike. When your child is in pain, it also gives you, as a parent, the beautiful opportunity to comfort them, and the child gets to feel the love and safety of their parent. It's the same with God. When you go to God in pain, God answers the pain with comfort and love.

LAYING THE DAILY GROUNDWORK TO RECEIVE GOD

One beautiful—and easy—way to embed our faith is to give thanks to God and show our gratitude every day. When it's as routine as brushing our teeth, it becomes second nature. So, we have words we say before we even get out of bed. We open our eyes and say:

MORNING PRAYER

I thank You, living and eternal King, for You have mercifully restored my soul within me. Great is Your faithfulness.

Hebrew:
מוֹדֶה אֲנִי לְפָנֶיךָ מֶלֶךְ חַי וְקַיָּם, שֶׁהֶחֱזַרְתָּ בִּי נִשְׁמָתִי בְּחֶמְלָה:
רַבָּה אֱמוּנָתֶךָ

In Hebrew transliterated:
Modeh ani lefanecha melech chai vekayam, she-he-chezarta bee nishmatee b'chemla, raba emunatecha.

This brief prayer ignites a daily conversation with God. It's not a one-way street. It's about connection and interaction. When a person recites a simple prayer—in that moment that they're engaging with God, and their entire body and soul are in complete unity with God—it sets a beautiful tone for the rest of the day.

NIKKI: You know, we've all heard this expression about being a "good Jew." Remember when Rowan said to you in the ICU that we're not good Jews because we're not observant, what does that mean to you?

RABBI ELI: Let me tell you a story that illustrates this beautifully. Not long ago, a man came to see me. He had grown up in the Soviet Union, where practising religion was forbidden, and now, as an adult, he was trying to learn more about Judaism. He'd been studying with great sincerity, but one day he turned to me and said, "Rabbi, I can't do this anymore."

I gently asked him what was troubling him. He said, "When I come to synagogue, I see everyone around me praying, singing, reading from the siddur [prayer book]—and I feel completely lost. I don't even know how to hold the prayer book the right way."

Knowing he'd lived through difficult times under Soviet rule, I invited him to tell me about his childhood. He shared a powerful memory:

When he was very young, his grandmother was secretly baking matzah (unleavened bread) for Passover—a dangerous act under Soviet law. This day, someone had informed the KGB, and officers came and banged loudly on the door. His quick-thinking grandmother ran to the bedroom and hid the matzah inside a pillowcase. Then she placed his potty in the middle of the room, told him to sit on it, and instructed him to cry loudly and not stop under any circumstances. His grandmother was not a woman to disobey, so he did what he was told.

The KGB burst in and accused her of making matzah. "We can smell it," they shouted. But as the little boy sat there wailing and sobbing, the agents grew agitated and uncomfortable. They told him to be quiet, but his grandmother was the law, and he carried on with her instructions. His crying distracted them so much that they eventually left—without searching the home or arresting his grandmother.

The cries of a dutiful grandson saved his grandmother's life—and saved the Passover matzah.

As he was sharing this with me all those years later, the man sat in my synagogue and had a sublime realisation. He said, *"That was my mitzvah! That's MY Judaism!"* And I told him: "Do you realise that at the tender age of five or six you risked your life for a piece of matzah? That single act, as a child, risked more for God than most people ever do in a lifetime. That moment, when you tapped into the very essence of your soul, catapulted you to a level where you were close to God in a way that many people only dream of. In God's eyes, you were more beautiful than the most knowledgeable rabbi.

So, there's no such thing as a "good Jew" or a "bad Jew," only that we're all human beings doing the best we can. It's not about how perfectly we say the words, but how earnestly we seek a connection with God when we do it.

NIKKI: Do you think we're living in a spiritual age? Or a distracted one?

RABBI ELI: Both. The Talmud teaches that in the days before the Messiah, the "knowledge of God will fill the world like the ocean covers the sea floor." We're living in that time.

Yes, we're surrounded by distractions—social media, celebrity culture, constant noise. But we also have more access to Torah, wisdom, and spiritual tools than ever before in history. And it's even available on Amazon.

NIKKI: In a fractured world where structured religion is less and less practiced and a universal moral order is perceptibly in decline, how do we teach our kids to believe in something beyond the material and the seen?

RABBI ELI: The Noahide Laws are the first port of call—they give us the rules and the inspiration. Then there are the daily, weekly, monthly, and yearly rituals (some of which we talked about) and they're an important scaffolding too. But crucially, and here's where we're talking about the first law in action, we need to teach our kids how to see beyond the material and tangible, to train the heart and mind, to see God and the miraculous in everything and every moment.

But maybe the most powerful way to help others is by being a **living example**. You can't say, "Do as I say, not as I do." If you love God, if you live with joy and purpose, your kids will see it. The world will see it. It's like putting on your oxygen mask first—you have to be lit up before you can share the flame.

FINAL THOUGHTS: THE ONE AND THE MANY

NIKKI: So . . . *who* is God and *why* should I worship Him?

RABBI ELI: There is only One true God. But we experience Him in many ways. There's the infinite, unknowable essence of God—*Ein Sof*. Then there are the ways He chooses to reveal Himself—through Torah, through the Noahide Laws, through nature, through justice, through compassion, through love—and through miracles. It's all the same Light. Just refracted through different lenses, like sunlight through stained glass.

God didn't create the world to remain distant. He made it to be discovered. He *wants* us to find Him. That's the pleasure of this whole game. That's the *why*!

NIKKI: You're saying faith isn't blind. It's vision.

RABBI ELI: Faith isn't about switching off your brain. It's about switching on your soul.

When you believe, you begin to see.

And when you see through God's eyes, you realise the world is not broken.

It's simply waiting.

CHAPTER 2

Why Are We So Afraid to Talk About God?

NOAHIDE LAW 2: DO NOT BLASPHEME (Speak Well)

Death and life are in the power of the tongue,
And those who love it will eat its fruit.

PROVERBS 18:21

ശ

THE ORIGINS OF THE SECOND LAW: DO NOT BLASPHEME

The second of the Seven Noahide Laws, *Do not blaspheme,* might be one of the most misunderstood. In the modern age of satire, sarcasm, and free speech, it's tempting to see this as a fusty, outdated taboo. But in Jewish tradition, blasphemy isn't about fragile gods sending lightning rods to strike you down or censorship. It's about reverence. It's about words—and the immense power they hold.

The origin of this law also comes from the **Book of Genesis**, and is reinforced in **Leviticus**, where God commands Moses:

> And whoever blasphemes the name of the Lord shall surely be put to death. All the congregation shall certainly stone him.
>
> —Leviticus 24:16

This severe consequence is less about punishing speech, and more about protecting and honouring something sacred: the awareness of God's name—and by extension, God's presence—is to be praised, not degraded.

However, this law actually has its roots in an even earlier period. When Adam is created, he is given the power to name all creatures—to use language not only to describe reality but to shape it. And when humanity later becomes corrupt before the flood, it is not just through violence but through the **breakdown of language** that society falls.

To blaspheme—to curse God, to speak of the Divine contemptuously—is seen in Jewish tradition as an act that fractures the bridge between heaven and earth.

But here's the profound truth: This law is not just about God. It's about how we speak *about anything* sacred—including each other. Blasphemy is a kind of spiritual vandalism. It tears at the fabric of what is holy. And holiness in Judaism is not remote. It is found in the human being, made in God's image.

"The power of speech," said Rabbi Eli, "is what separates us from every other creature. It can build worlds—or destroy them."

When the Talmud teaches that the Second Noahide Law prohibits cursing God, it's also asking us: How do you speak about the sacred? How do you bless God? Do your words honour or degrade? Do they lift up or pull down?

In today's world—with digital shouting matches played out in real time on social media, anonymous comment threads, and the weaponisation of words—this law is, instead of being outdated, more relevant than ever. To make a conscious decision not to blaspheme is to speak with care. To understand that language is never neutral. To know that reverence begins with restraint, and the understanding that our words have the power to connect us to God and to each other.

A NOTE ON OUR CONVERSATION

I don't know when I first became afraid to talk about God out loud. Maybe it was at primary school where I was taunted for being a Christ-killer at the tender age of eight years old. Or perhaps it was growing up in a secular Jewish family where culture was proudly embraced, but belief was . . . well, complicated.

My dad had gone to a Catholic boarding school and had become one of the fastest runners there. Was he trying to outrun the bullies, or was he secretly trying to outrun being Jewish? His father was a small-time crook who was often in the newspapers for petty crimes, owning illegal bars, and dubious financial dealings. Dad was ashamed of him and felt he was tarred with the old Jewish moneylender brush.

My mother, a refined and fashionable woman who loved clothes and expensive jewellery, attended the most exclusive girls' school in Melbourne. Her German Jewish parents were traumatised by the Holocaust and determined to integrate into secular Australian life.

With parents who did not grow up Jewish and in fact thought of themselves as Australian first, and Jewish not even a close second, I grew up knowing very little about my religion or culture.

But I was a serious child, and I remember I prayed. Quietly. Sometimes fervently. But because the family wasn't religious, I never really talked about it.

Even as an adult, when I found myself in crisis—at my father's deathbed or about to be intubated and induced into a coma on the edge of life and death—I didn't pray in formal Jewish words.

I just reached and hoped. A whisper from the part of me that deeply believed there was something sacred behind the veil.

When I met Rabbi Eli Schlanger, I found myself in the presence of someone who not only talked about God openly and eagerly—he lived with God, breathed God, wrestled with God. He was not afraid to use the word. He was not afraid to love it. He was not afraid to fear it either.

Everyone who knew Eli felt as though they were in the presence of someone quite special. He was the first person to say he wasn't a saint, but not many people walk with God in a moment-by-moment real-time way. It made him electric, somewhat eccentric, and very alive. He told me the other rabbis called him a "rough diamond," which he liked because it reflected his authenticity and knockabout charm. He had the rare gift of being able to get onto anyone's level in nanoseconds, whether they be a prime minister or a prisoner. He was a teacher by example, not words. He used his thoughts and deeds as a way to reflect God's grace in the world and it's for that reason that he'll be so missed.

In this conversation, we discussed the **power of words**, the **mystery of names**, and the Jewish perspective on something that makes many modern people very uncomfortable: **reverence**.

The Second Noahide Law is often translated as "Do not curse God." That sounds strange, archaic, almost medieval. But Eli expanded on the thought: "as a deep call to understand the **weight of speech**, the **sacredness of naming**, and the way our words **either elevate or diminish** the world."

As we spoke, I realised how much of our casual modern speech is laced with blasphemy—not in the fire-and-brimstone way, but in the way we flatten awe, trivialise truth, and toss around words that were once considered holy. This chapter isn't about censorship. It's about sacred attention.

What do we say? What do we mean?

And who are we, really, when we speak of God?

∽

NIKKI: Hey Eli, you're in your car. Where are you going?

RABBI ELI: I'm going to the local prison.

NIKKI: So, how many Jews are there in the local prison?

RABBI ELI: There's just one. And I've got my shofar ready to awaken my soul!

NIKKI: (Laughing) Your soul is already awakened, Eli. What about the prisoner's soul?

RABBI ELI: You know, a lot of people ask me why I go to visit prisons. It is a fair way away, but one Jew is important in a country where there are so few of us. I don't judge what he's done; we don't talk about it. It's an opportunity to talk about God.

NIKKI: You never know when someone will have a complete awakening. It doesn't matter if they're a celebrity or a prisoner; anyone can awaken at any moment.

RABBI ELI: God has given us all a particular mission in life. By talking about God to this man in prison, I'm also giving him an opportunity to elevate and inspire the people around him. Every stone thrown into the pond ripples outwards. Our words have meaning. Our words have effects. Our words have power.

NIKKI: The Second Noahide Law is often translated as "Do not curse God," but that wording sits awkwardly with me. It sounds like something from the Dark Ages. What does it really mean?

RABBI ELI: You're right to question the language. Even in traditional texts, we don't use the phrase "curse God"—it's too jarring, too contradictory. Instead, we use a euphemism: "Don't bless God," which is understood to mean the opposite. Remember, we discussed *leshon sagi nahor* in our last conversation. Jewish tradition teaches us that speech isn't just descriptive; it's creative. Our words shape the world.

NIKKI: That really resonates. In so many spiritual traditions, the world begins with a word.

RABBI ELI: Exactly. And that's the crux of this law. It's not just about blaspheming or cursing—it's about our reverence for the sacredness of words. Understanding that the words we use to speak about God, about life, about each other—those words have weight. They can carry light or darkness. It's up to us how we use them.

Human beings are the only creatures on Earth with the power of conscious speech. Animals have instincts, intelligence, even emotion—but speech? That's Divine. When we speak, we're not just expressing thoughts—we're *bringing them into being.*

NIKKI: When I say, "I'm writing a book," it suddenly exists beyond my brain. It starts taking shape.

RABBI ELI: That's it. You're co-creating. First, the spark of inspiration—that's wisdom. Then understanding—wrestling with the idea, turning it over in your mind. But the moment it comes out of your mouth or lands on the page, it becomes a real thing.

Positive speech, holy speech, and prayer, our Sages tell us, create angels. The intention behind our words is very powerful and it helps cement our reverence for God. It's our offering to Him. This intentional positive speech fills the world with goodness and holy light.

The flip side is evil speech—*lashon hara*, gossip or slander. When we speak negatively about someone, we're not just saying something benign and neutral, we're unleashing energy, creating harm, even if the person never hears it.

NIKKI: You're saying the damage still lands even if the words never reach that person's ears.

RABBI ELI: Not only does it land—it lingers. The Talmud says that when we speak lashon hara, we harm three people: the one we're talking about, the one we're speaking to, and ourselves. Even if the subject never hears a word, they feel it on a soul level. Words are vibrations. They ripple through the fabric of the world.

NIKKI: I've been thinking a lot about this lately, especially when I see those horrific chants on social media like "Death to Jews," coming from children, from crowds. It's not just political rhetoric. It *hurts*. Physically, emotionally, spiritually.

RABBI ELI: It's spiritual violence. It doesn't matter how young someone is or how rehearsed the slogan might be. When those words leave a mouth, they carry spiritual consequence. And yes—it hurts, even if we pretend we're used to it. We're not.

But we also have to remember: Their words are rooted in falsehood. And lies, by their very nature, don't last.

NIKKI: You've said that to me before—truth has legs.

RABBI ELI: Let me explain something beautiful from Hebrew. The word for truth is *emet*—אמת. Three letters: *aleph*, *mem*, and *tav*. All of them stand firmly on two legs. Stable. Balanced.

But the word for falsehood is *sheker*—שקר. *Shin*, *kuf*, and *resh*. Each of those letters balances on one leg. Wobbly. Temporary. Truth endures. Lies collapse under their own weight.

That's why we're still here. The Babylonians, the Romans, the Nazis—they were mighty empires. But they crumbled. Why? Because they were built on lies. The Jewish people are still standing because our foundation is truth, and at the heart of that truth is God.

NIKKI: So even truth isn't truth without God?

RABBI ELI: Yes, correct, and you're right to push me. I should have said, truth doesn't exist without God. Take the Hebrew word *emet* again. That first letter, *aleph,* represents God. It's the first letter of the Hebrew alphabet and has a numerical value of one. Unity. The Source. Now take God out of *emet.* What are you left with?

NIKKI: *Met*?

RABBI ELI: *Met* means death. You remove the Divine from truth, and all that remains is emptiness. That's the core of this commandment—not just "Don't curse God," but don't strip the sacred out of your speech. Don't make your mouth a factory of hollow words. In fact, you're given the power to do the exact opposite. Through intention and prayer, we each have the ability to bless God, not curse; to revere; to bring light not darkness.

NIKKI: It's such a powerful concept. It calls on all of us to become super conscious of what comes out of our mouths. And even before words are formed, what we think and concentrate on.

RABBI ELI: That's why this law matters. Because the world we're in now is saturated with words—posts, tweets, headlines, hashtags—but so much of it is disconnected from truth, from responsibility, from reverence. This commandment isn't about censorship. It's about consciousness. It's about asking ourselves: *When I speak, am I adding light to the world, or subtracting it?*

NIKKI: Why are people uncomfortable talking about God? I know for myself that it's not something I am open about in polite society . . . Or maybe it's just that as a secular Jew, my society isn't used to talking about God as part of everyday conversation.

RABBI ELI: Deep down, we know God is not just a word; that word is a door. And we're afraid of what might be behind it. We live in a time when people are more comfortable discussing energy, the universe, and even "spirituality." But say the word "God," and suddenly people get awkward. Why? Because "God" implies accountability. It means someone is watching. It suggests there's actually a right and a wrong.

That's confronting.

That's challenging.

NIKKI: As we discussed in the previous chapter, we're coy about using the name of God, but I'm wondering if all this cloak-and-dagger stuff about the word doesn't somehow separate us from God? Isn't naming part of connecting?

RABBI ELI: The name of God is not just a label. It's a vibration. A frequency. A spark of holiness. So we treat it with tremendous care.

There's a teaching in Pirkei Avot: "Be careful with your words." It's not just about politeness. It's about energy. Words create worlds. And names—especially Divine names—hold untold spiritual power.

That's why in the Jewish tradition, we don't say the true name of God, the Tetragrammaton, out loud. We use alternatives—like *Hashem*, meaning "the Name."

It's not superstition. It's reverence. It's respect. It's remembering.

NIKKI: So, the Second Noahide Law, "Do not curse God"—how do we make sense of that today?

RABBI ELI: First, it's not just about swearing or using God's name in vain. It's about something deeper: recognising the **sanctity of speech**.

Blasphemy, in the Torah sense, is when you strip away the holiness of something. When you degrade the sacred. When you use language to disconnect instead of to elevate.

So, the real heart of this law is: *Don't diminish the Divine with your words. Don't treat holiness like it's disposable. Instead, use your words to connect you to God, to uplift everything—yourself and the world.*

NIKKI: That's powerful. But what about people who don't believe in God? Does this law still matter?

RABBI ELI: Absolutely. Because even if you don't consciously believe in the idea of God, most people have an intrinsic belief in something.

The way we speak about our values, about life, about each other . . . it all flows from the same spiritual principle: that **speech shapes reality**.

We may not be conscious of it all the time, but we feel it in our bodies, our bones, and our guts when we say awful things about other people. And when we deny that feeling, it submerges and goes somewhere dark and hidden. And just as easily, bringing reverence to the words you use brings us closer to God, even if one doesn't consciously believe in Him.

So, yes, this law matters to everyone. Because, when you honour speech, you honour life.

NIKKI: You said, "Speech is the soul made visible." That sentence is sticky, powerful, profound; it holds a lot of truth for me.

RABBI ELI: Because it IS true. The first thing God does in the Torah is *speak*. "Let there be light." And there was light. Creation begins with speech. And every time we speak, we're creating something—light or darkness.

NIKKI: How do we use speech in a holy way? In a modern life full of texts, posts, emails, and endless talk?

RABBI ELI: Start with awareness. Ask yourself before you speak: *Is this true? Is this kind? Is this necessary?*

Judaism has a beautiful term: *lashon hakodesh*—"the holy tongue." It reminds us that speech is sacred. That's why we pray with our mouths. That's why gossip is so harmful. That's why blessings are so powerful.

Every word leaves an indelible imprint on the canvas of the world.

NIKKI: And what about prayer? I've often struggled with prayer. I didn't want to pray to the Hollywood notion of a man with a white beard on a throne in the sky. Instinctively, I reviled that.

I recoiled from it. But when I do pray, I wonder if I'm really just talking to myself.

RABBI ELI: That's okay. You're not alone in that.

Prayer is not about perfect language. It's about opening a channel. Sometimes silence is prayer. Sometimes tears. Sometimes, just breathing with intention.

But here's the secret: Prayer isn't only for God. It's for you. It aligns your soul. It reminds you who you are. It teaches you to listen—not just speak.

NIKKI: And yet some people mock prayer. Or say it's delusional. What would you tell them?

RABBI ELI: I'd say that cynicism is a cheap substitute for wonder.

Prayer is not weakness. It's the ultimate act of courage—to speak from your soul, even when you're not sure anyone is listening.

And deep down, everyone is praying. Breathing is praying. Living is praying. The thoughts in our head when we're wishing for something better are prayers. Even the atheist who cries out in the dark when something terrible happens—that's a prayer. It's raw. It's real.

It's sublimely human, yet it reaches beyond us.

NIKKI: You told me a story once about a woman who was sick, and how she changed just from starting to say a blessing. Can you share it here?

RABBI ELI: Yes. She had stage four cancer and was very resistant to anything religious. Her family begged me to come.

At first, she wouldn't even let me in the room. But eventually, I offered her one small thing: to say a daily blessing over water. Just that.

"*Baruch Atah Hashem . . . shehakol nihyeh bidvaro*—Blessed are You, God . . . through whose word all came to be."

She rolled her eyes at first. But then she started doing it. And she told me, "I don't know if it's doing anything for God—but it's doing something to me."

Blessings do that. They *recalibrate the soul.*

NIKKI: I love that. It's not about proving anything to God—it's about softening the heart.

RABBI ELI: Exactly. And that's what this law is about. Not fear. Not censorship. Not control.

It's about remembering that seemingly mundane, everyday things—like what we say and think—are holy—and treating them as such.

The First Noahide Law is to believe in the one God and the unity and sanctity of God. We each have this direct relationship in which God focuses on us with intense attention.

NIKKI: So this obviously relates a lot to prayer. We're not reaching God's ears via a prophet or man; we go directly to the Source, right?

RABBI ELI: Excellent. Excellent. The core of the prayer was a commandment or mitzvah given to us to speak directly to God in times of need. God wants us to talk to Him. God wants us to relate to Him as humans, and human relationships are built through communication, specifically verbal communication.

NIKKI: You told me a beautiful story about your daughter asking about prayer. Please tell me again.

RABBI ELI: Of course. One night, I was saying the *Shema* with my daughter Priva before bed—she would have been about three years old at the time. It was a nightly ritual for us—one of the holiest prayers in Judaism, declaring the oneness of God.

She looked up at me, big brown eyes full of curiosity, and said, "Tatty, why do we have to say this every day? Doesn't God already know what we want?"

I smiled. "That's an excellent question." Priva paused for a moment and then followed it with something even deeper: "If God knows everything, why are we telling Him anything?"

And she's right. That's the heart of the matter.

I told her: "We're not saying the *Shema* for God's sake. We're saying it for ours."

Prayer isn't to inform God of anything. He already knows. Prayer is to remind us of who we are, of what matters, of the truth we forget in the rush of the day, and to connect with Him.

NIKKI: That's such a powerful reframe. It's not about pleading with the universe . . . It's about aligning ourselves.

RABBI ELI: The *Shema* starts with, "*Hear, O Israel.*" It's not "Speak, O Israel." It begins with hearing. With *listening*. Before we talk, before we ask, before we cry out . . . we listen. Prayer isn't about noise. It's about presence.

And sometimes a child's question reveals more than a thousand sermons.

THE *SHEMA*

Cover your eyes with your right hand and say:
Listen, Israel: the Lord is our God, the Lord is One.

Recite the following verse in an undertone:
Blessed be the name of His glorious kingdom forever and all time.

Love the Lord your God with all your heart, with all your soul, and with all your might. These words which I command you today shall be on your heart. Teach them to your children repeatedly, speaking of them when you sit at home and when you travel on the way, when you lie down and when you rise. Bind them as a sign on your hand, and they shall be an emblem between your eyes. Write them on the doorposts of your house and gates.

Cover your eyes with your right hand and say:
שְׁמַע יִשְׂרָאֵל יְ-ה-וָ-ה אֱלֹקֵינוּ יְ-ה-וָ-ה אֶחָד:

Recite the following verse in an undertone:
בָּרוּךְ שֵׁם כְּבוֹד מַלְכוּתוֹ לְעוֹלָם וָעֶד:

וְאָהַבְתָּ אֵת יְ-הֹ-וָ-ה אֱלֹהֶיךָ בְּכָל־לְבָבְךָ וּבְכָל־נַפְשְׁךָ וּבְכָל־
מְאֹדֶךָ: וְהָיוּ הַדְּבָרִים הָאֵלֶּה אֲשֶׁר אָנֹכִי מְצַוְּךָ הַיּוֹם עַל־לְבָבֶךָ:
וְשִׁנַּנְתָּם לְבָנֶיךָ וְדִבַּרְתָּ בָּם בְּשִׁבְתְּךָ בְּבֵיתֶךָ וּבְלֶכְתְּךָ בַדֶּרֶךְ
וּבְשָׁכְבְּךָ וּבְקוּמֶךָ: וּקְשַׁרְתָּם לְאוֹת עַל־יָדֶךָ וְהָיוּ לְטֹטָפֹת בֵּין
עֵינֶיךָ: וּכְתַבְתָּם עַל מְזֻזוֹת בֵּיתֶךָ וּבִשְׁעָרֶיךָ:

Cover your eyes with your right hand and say:
Shemah yeesrah-eyl ah-doh-nai eh-loh-hay-noo ah-doh-nai eh-khahd.

Recite the following verse in an undertone:
Bah-rookh shem ki-vohd mahl-khoo-toh li-oh-lahm vah-ehd.

Vah-hahv-tah ayt ah-doh-noi eh-loh-heh-khah bi-khohl li-vahv-khah, oov-khohl nahf-shkhah, oov-khohl moh-deh-khah. Vi-hah-yoo hahd-vah-reem hah-ay-leh, ah-shehr ah-noh-khee mi-tzah-vi-khah hah-yohm ahl li-vah-veh-khah. Vi-shee-nahn-tahm li-vah-neh-khah vi-dee-bahr-tah bahm bi-sheev-tkhah bi-vay-teh-khah, oov-lekht-khah vah-deh-rekh, oov-shah-khbkhah oov-koo-meh-khah. Ook-shahr-tahm loht ahl yah-deh-khah, vi-hah-yoo li-toh-tah-foht bayn ay-neh-khah. Ookh-tahv-tahm ahl mi-zoo-zoht bay-teh-khah oo-vee-shah-reh-khah.

NIKKI: So if the First Noahide Law is about *who* we worship, the second feels like it's about how we talk about that relationship. "Do not blaspheme" sounds very medieval to most people—like shouting curses at the sky. But what about the quiet stuff? The dark thoughts, the gossip, the rage, the hate speech. Does all of that fall under this law?

RABBI ELI: In a deep sense, yes.

On the most basic level, the rabbis define the Second Noahide Law as a prohibition on **"birkas Hashem"**—literally "blessing God," used as a euphemism for *cursing* or explicitly rejecting God. Classical sources understand this reverence as a **universal expectation**, a fundamental pillar of any relationship with the Creator.

But if you zoom out a little, blasphemy isn't only a sentence you shout. It's a whole *posture* of the mouth and mind: How easily do I spit contempt—at God, at people made in God's image, at myself?

SPEECH AS A "GARMENT" OF THE SOUL

NIKKI: Okay, but how does Kabbalah see all this? Because "don't curse God" still feels very narrow compared to our messy reality.

RABBI ELI: Kabbalah widens it beautifully.

The Tanya teaches that the soul expresses itself through **three "garments": thought, speech, and action.** They're called garments because you can put them on and take them off; they're not *you*, but they reveal you. When the soul "wears" holy thoughts, words, and deeds, it shines; when it "wears" ugly ones, it gets covered in spiritual grime.

Literally, this second law is about **not turning your mouth and mind into an idol factory.** It asks:

> *Which God are you talking about: the real One—or a distorted caricature you've built in your head? And how do your words about other people quietly deny the image of God in them?*

LASHON HARA: WHEN SPEECH BECOMES SPIRITUAL POISON

NIKKI: Let's talk about gossip. Because most of us don't stand on a street corner cursing God by name. We share WhatsApps and TikToks.

RABBI ELI: The classic name for this in Jewish law is **lashon hara**—"evil speech." The Torah roots it in verses like "You shall not go about as a talebearer among your people" (Leviticus 19:16), and "You shall not circulate a false report" (Exodus 23:1).

From there, a vast literature develops—culminating in Rabbi Yisrael Meir ha-Kohen Kagan (1838–1933), who was known as the **Chafetz Chaim**, and his work on guarding the tongue. He showed that one careless sentence can break multiple Torah prohibitions at once. He even writes that this sin "corrupts all worlds and darkens their light"—very Kabbalistic language for "you've just messed with the spiritual wiring of reality."

The **Zohar** goes further: It links evil speech to the **"sin of the serpent"** and suggests that **lashon hara** activates very dark spiritual forces. In some passages, it says that God can forgive many things, but **lashon hara** is terrifyingly hard to repair.

NIKKI: So blasphemy isn't only when I scream "I hate God" in traffic; it's also when I casually shred someone's reputation at brunch?

RABBI ELI: Yes, because you're degrading someone who carries the **Divine image**. If blasphemy is contempt for God, **lashon hara** is contempt for God's **likeness** reflected in other people.

ANGER AS MINI-IDOLATRY

NIKKI: What about those volcanic moments—you know, when you say things you "don't really mean," but you *did*?

RABBI ELI: The tradition is brutally honest here. The Talmud and later Maimonides say that **one who gives in to anger is "as if he worshipped idols."**

Chasidic philosophy explains why: Pure rage is a moment when you **erase God from the scene.** You act as if there is no grace, no providence, no bigger story—only your wounded ego and its right to explode. For those seconds, anger is the only god in the room.

So, yes, a screaming, hateful outburst can be a kind of *emotional blasphemy*: not necessarily because you cursed God's name explicitly, but because you denied His presence with your whole nervous system and your soul.

PRACTICES THAT GUARD THE SECOND LAW

NIKKI: All right, Eli, this is making me a bit nervous about opening my mouth at all. What do we *do* with this? How does an ordinary person actually work with this Law in daily life?

RABBI ELI: Let's talk practices again—this time for the **second** law.

1. Transformative Speech: Using the Mouth as a Light-Source

RABBI ELI: Kabbalah is big on **tikkun**—repair. It doesn't just say "don't" talk badly. It asks, *"What will you do instead?"*

One of the beautiful ideas you find in later sources is that **Torah study and words of blessing, spoken out loud, are the tikkun for lashon hara.** When you use your tongue to learn wisdom, to bless, to comfort, you are re-dedicating the "organ of speech" to its original Owner.

Simple practices:

- Say a **short blessing** before and after eating, even in your own language.
- Get into the habit of **saying thank you out loud**—to people and to God.
- Read a few lines of **Tehillim (Psalms)** or some teaching each day *with your voice*, not just your eyes.

NIKKI: So the idea is that my mouth is never neutral. It's either darkening the world or bringing light to it.

RABBI ELI: Exactly. In Kabbalistic language, every word is either dressing your soul in *light* or in *klipah*—a shell that hides God.

2. Shemirat HaLashon: A Daily Speech Practice

RABBI ELI: There's a whole modern discipline called **Shemirat HaLashon**—"Guarding the tongue."

A few very practical moves:

- **Daily learning:** The aim is to reprogram the "speech garment" of your soul, and teach your mouth what it's for.
- **The pause rule:** Before saying something about another person, you silently ask three questions:
  - Is it true?
  - Is it necessary?
  - Is it kind or at least constructive?

If it fails the test, you let the sentence die on your tongue. That tiny act of *withholding* is a spiritual achievement; you've just kept your mouth from violating the image of God in someone else.

NIKKI: I'm getting the picture. Every time I *don't* send the snarky text, I'm keeping the second law?

RABBI ELI: You're certainly walking in its spirit: refusing to turn your speech into a weapon against what God cares about.

3. Anger Work: From Outburst to Prayer

NIKKI: And what about those "I'm-done-with-God" moments? The bitterness, the urge to slam the door on the whole relationship?

RABBI ELI: First, Judaism doesn't ask you to pretend you never feel that. The Bible is full of people who argue with God—**Job, Jeremiah, the authors of Psalms.** Their greatness lies in bringing protest *into* the relationship rather than walking away from it.

Practically, a few tools:

- NAME IT, DON'T NARRATE IT. When you feel rage rising, you say—even quietly: "I am feeling furious right now." That's very different from launching into a story about how the universe or this person is evil and against you.
- TURN THE OUTBURST INTO A PSALM. Instead of "God, I hate you," try: "God, I'm in so much pain I *want* to hate

You. Show me how to heal." That's not blasphemy; that's raw prayer.

- **BREATH AS KABBALISTIC MEDICINE.** The word for "soul" (*neshama*) is linked to "breath" (*neshima*). The Kabbalists point out that anger is *short breath—kotzer ruach.* Lengthening the breath is literally giving your soul back some space so it can retake the wheel.

NIKKI: So even when I'm on the edge of cursing God, there's a way to shift that from blasphemy into a brutally honest psalm?

RABBI ELI: Exactly. The second law does not say, "Never *feel* negativity." It's saying, "Don't harden that negativity into a theology of contempt." Keep it fluid, keep it in conversation.

4. Zero-Tolerance Zones for Hate Speech

RABBI ELI: One more very concrete area: hate speech.

If every human carries the Divine image, then **dehumanising language** skates dangerously close to spiritual desecration. It says, effectively: "This kind of person is outside the circle of sacredness."

A spiritual practice here is to declare specific phrases, slurs, and generalisations **off-limits.** A conversation reframe might be:

I'm trying to be more careful with my words. Can we talk about this without that language?

That's a quiet fulfilment of the second law: refusing to let God's name—or God's image—be dragged through the mud in your corner of the world.

NIKKI: And what about those times when people want to argue with you? Being Jewish is in itself controversial these days.

RABBI ELI: You can't ultimately change people's minds. If they're going to hate you, they're going to hate you. But if they're open to a conversation, and you're open to a conversation, you can use it as an opportunity to share God's light. After all, that's what we're here for, to be a vessel of God's light.

THE INNER QUESTION OF THE SECOND LAW

NIKKI: So if I strip all this down, what is the Second Noahide Law really asking me, day to day?

RABBI ELI: Maybe something like this:

In your thoughts and your words—about God, about others, about yourself—you have the choice to speak as though the world is godless, or as if every moment is filled with Presence.

Blasphemy, in its most profound sense, isn't only a forbidden sentence. It's a way of thinking and speaking that erases holiness—from God's Name, from people's names, from your own name.

Every time you choose restraint over gossip, prayer over a curse, a long breath over a screamed insult—Kabbalah would say you're not just being polite. You're **realigning the garments of your soul** with the One whose Name you carry.

And that, in the language of our book, is another way of saying: You're learning to talk like someone who knows they live in God's world.

FINAL THOUGHTS ON THE SACRED POWER OF OUR WORDS

NIKKI: This conversation shook something loose in me.

It could be because, like so many modern people, I've used spiritual words lightly. Carelessly. I've said "Oh my God" without thought, and I've sent OMG texts and emojis far too often. Sometimes, I'm embarrassed to admit, I've prayed only when I was desperate.

I never meant harm. But I never really meant reverence either.

And yet . . . when you speak about *speech*, I feel something ancient stir inside me. A memory. A knowing.

RABBI ELI: It's crucial for us to remember that our words matter. That naming is powerful. That silence, too, is sacred.

NIKKI: What it sparks in me is that in a time when truth feels so cheap and language so weaponised, this second law—this invitation, this utterance [as Eli calls it]—is more relevant than ever.

Speak with care.

Speak with courage.

And leave room for God to speak back.

CHAPTER 3

What If People Are Just . . . Terrible?

NOAHIDE LAW 3: DO NOT MURDER (Choose Life)

I have set before you life and death . . . *choose life.*

DEUTERONOMY 30:19

ര

THE ORIGINS OF THE THIRD LAW: DO NOT MURDER

The commandment *not to murder* is the third of the Seven Noahide Laws—the moral code given by God to Noah after the flood for all of humanity. It seems obvious that a prohibition on murder is foundational to all societies . . . and yet it's not. Not all societies have and abide by the religious and legal structures that prevent the taking of human life. It's more complex than a superficial glance might suggest.

The Seventh Noahide Law, which dictates the setting up of courts and legal frameworks to protect citizens, gives this law even more power and intention.

While often mistaken as a rule solely from the Ten Commandments given to Moses at Sinai, the prohibition against murder predates Sinai. It is a foundational principle that appears in Genesis, where God tells Noah:

> Whoever sheds man's blood, By man his blood shall be shed; For in the image of God He made man.
>
> —Genesis 9:6

This verse establishes three critical ideas:

1. **HUMAN LIFE IS SACRED**—because every person is made *b'tzelem Elokim*—in the image of God.

2. **TAKING A LIFE IS A COSMIC OFFENCE**—not just a crime against society but an assault on God's presence in the world.
3. **THERE MUST BE JUSTICE**—not vengeance, but moral accountability.

Historically, this commandment became the bedrock of moral civilisation and our Judeo-Christian legal and ethical systems. But it was not merely a social contract; it was a Divine edict that safeguarded life as sacred. In a world rebuilding itself after the flood, this law reminded humanity that chaos and violence must be restrained by reverence and responsibility.

Judaism—and by extension the Noahide system, which was re-delivered to Moses at Sinai—draws a distinction between **murder** (intentional, unlawful killing) and **killing** (which may include self-defence, warfare, or accidental death). The law condemns not just the act but also the *hatred and dehumanisation* that lead to it.

As Rabbi Eli said, "The moment we forget that life is Divine, we open the door to darkness."

This law challenges us not only to *refrain from murder*, but to *actively honour life*—to treat others with dignity, and to build societies that reflect the sanctity of every soul.

A NOTE ON OUR CONVERSATION

When Eli and I talked, it felt as though we were in a protected bubble. The bubble burst when Eli was killed. (NOTE: At the time of writing, I am constrained to using only the word "killed," due to legal instruction arising from ongoing court proceedings in Australia.)

It seems chillingly ironic that we talked about murder in abstract and spiritual terms in these circumstances and then Eli was actually . . . "killed." Even the word shakes me to my core. How do I come to terms with this senseless, violent, appalling act? I long for a conversation with Eli, my spiritual North, to show me a path to healing and peace with it. Right now, as I write this, only three days after the shooting, my guts are churning, my pulse is racing, I'm sweating, and I'm trying valiantly to hold back tears.

Eli knew the risks of being an out and proud Jew, but nothing would deter him from that course. I confess now that I had harboured secret fears for his safety. Once or twice, I voiced those fears, but he believed he was Divinely protected. More importantly, he believed that life isn't confined to the body; it is eternal, infinite, and beyond time and space. That belief inspired a sense of awe in those who met him, as it seemed his body was a small container for something vast, indescribable, powerful, and eternal.

I imagine he would have said his death was ultimately God's will, that he would have accepted his fate. That said, Eli was also a father, husband, brother, friend, and minister to his community, so his responsibilities to those roles and people would have weighed heavily on him had he known he was departing so soon.

Reflecting on this topic now, I see that I have only one path. Eli's path. A path of love, light, forgiveness, wisdom, and peace.

Have I come to terms with his death? That's a resounding NO! I'm human, and I have to take time to process the trauma. But in all the months of all our conversations, Eli has changed me. Profoundly.

I started wearing a Magen David (Star of David) after October 7. I wasn't just wearing it as a symbol of my faith, but also as a talisman against the arrows, both literal and energetic, that come your way as a Jew walking around in the world. After what's happened to Eli, I am conscious of wearing it as the "**Shield of David**" (its literal translation). I NEED its mystical protection. I have, at times, caught people in shops looking at it, probably confused, wondering why this blond-haired, blue-eyed white-passing woman is wearing a Jewish star at her throat.

But Eli's influence on me stretches way beyond wearing the Magen David; I am wearing my Jewish identity in a new way. There are two reasons for this: Eli's miracle and my second chance at life invigorated my faith in God (anyone who's had a near-death experience will tell you that it changes you forever and that when there's no clear scientific reason for something, humans reach for the mystical and magical to explain it). And now, more importantly, Eli was killed, and I will never be the same.

At the outset, Eli set the mission for this book to bring light to the world—to elevate, uplift, inspire, and encourage the reader. We dove deep, and neither of us hesitated to ask hard questions or search for difficult answers.

Reading this is going to challenge some people. So I'll say right here and right now, go easy, be gentle, take pauses, and understand that these Noahide Laws are more important than ever. I encourage you to try to understand them. Especially the spiritual and ethical dimensions that Rabbi Eli took time to explain.

This chapter isn't about the end of life; it's about the burgeoning of hope and the deep connections we all have to life.

RABBI ELI: Let's start simple. In Judaism, life is not just sacred—it is Divine. Every human being, regardless of background, belief, or behaviour, carries a spark of the Divine. We say that every person is created *b'tzelem Elokim*, in the image of God. That's not just poetic. That's law. That's foundation.

Murder, therefore, is not only an act of violence against a human being. It is an act of violence against God Himself.

So "Do not murder" isn't just about avoiding bloodshed. It's about learning to see the *infinite potential* inside every human being. It's about reverence. It's about the love of God, and by extension, the love of humanity.

It's not just a legal line in the sand—it's a worldview. We're not allowed to devalue life in any form. That's why Jewish ethics are so strong around the unborn, around end-of-life decisions, and even around how we speak about people. Because murder starts with dehumanisation. The Torah makes it very clear—we're made in God's image. Once you forget that, that every individual is an embodiment of God in the world, dreadful things become possible. That's when societies fall.

NIKKI: But how do we value human life—even in war?

RABBI ELI: There's no glorification of violence in Judaism. War is not desirable. It's necessary in certain circumstances, but always with limits. We're told not to needlessly destroy trees in war. Think about that—if a tree matters, how much more a human being?

And we don't celebrate death. Not even the death of our enemies. When the angels wanted to sing after the Egyptians drowned in the sea, God said no—"My handiwork is drowning." That's the Jewish heart. Even in conflict, we don't lose our compassion.

NIKKI: I had always thought the Third Noahide Law—"Do not murder"—was the easiest to accept. Of course we shouldn't kill each other. But the more I sat with it, especially in the wake of rising antisemitism, rhetoric of extermination, and the way people casually degrade each other online, the more I understood this Law was about sacred compassion and universal love. The Jewish worldview does not see life merely as a biological fact, but as a spiritual charge—a Divine spark that comes with responsibility. And suddenly, I have questions. What about emotional cruelty? Is assisted dying murder? What about those who do seem irredeemably terrible?

RABBI ELI: To take emotional cruelty first, when we embarrass someone publicly, for example, the Talmud says it's like spilling blood. When we speak cruelly, degrade, or isolate others, we're participating in a kind of spiritual violence. It may not show up in court, but it registers in Heaven.

NIKKI: So hurtful words—especially when we dehumanise or vilify others—can carry that same moral weight?

RABBI ELI: Yes. Our words can kill spirit, hope, and connection.

NIKKI: Or ideas? Or reputations, or a child's sense of safety?

RABBI ELI: Absolutely. The Torah speaks directly to that. There's a concept in Judaism called *halbanat panim*—literally, "whitening someone's face"—and it refers to public humiliation. Our sages say that if you publicly embarrass someone, it is as if you spilled their blood. That's not a metaphor. That's spiritual anatomy.

Speech, too, can kill. Words have the power to create or destroy. The entire universe was created with speech—"And God said, let there be light."

When we speak cruelly, especially about others, we commit lashon hara—evil speech. And the Talmud says that this harms *three* people: the one who says it, the one who hears it, and the one it's about. Even if they never know. Even if they never hear.

NIKKI: That makes social media a spiritual minefield.

RABBI ELI: Exactly. People think gossip is harmless. But in Jewish thought, gossip is a terrible sin. It can destroy lives without a single weapon. It spreads like wildfire. And it desensitises us to the sacredness of each other.

NIKKI: So how do Jews stay moral when surrounded by antisemitism or threats?

RABBI ELI: This is personal. Right now, we're seeing an explosion of hate. And the Jewish people are hurting.

But Torah doesn't say, "Be holy when life is easy." It says *Kedoshim tihiyu*—you shall be holy—always. Even under pressure. Even when the world turns its back on you.

NIKKI: That feels impossible sometimes.

RABBI ELI: And yet, we must. Because if we lose our morality, we lose our mission.

The challenge is not to become what we fight. The challenge is to stay human, stay holy, even when others aren't. Our ancestors knew pogroms. The Shoah. Crusades. And yet we kept lighting candles. We kept teaching our children. We didn't curse the world. We blessed it.

We've had thousands of years of practice. We're not new to this. From Egypt to the Spanish Inquisition to the Nazis—we've faced hatred. But we've always clung to life. We cling to light. That's why Shabbat is such a powerful act. It's a declaration that life is worth celebrating.

And we also educate. We teach our kids that just because someone hates us, we don't hate back. That's hard. But it's holy. That's what makes us different.

NIKKI: Part of me goes, "Well . . . obviously no one should murder." Every religion says that, right?

RABBI ELI: You're right that it sounds obvious. But the Torah doesn't just say, "Murder is bad." It gives a *reason* that becomes the core of this view of life.

For the Noahide covenant, the key verse comes after the flood. God tells Noah that whoever sheds human blood will be held accountable "*for in the image of God He made man.*"

So, the prohibition on murder is not just "don't harm society." It's: **Don't attack the image of God.**

That's already a very holy way of framing it.

"YOU KILL A WORLD"

NIKKI: Okay, but what does it *mean* to kill the image of God? Because humans don't exactly look Divine most of the time.

RABBI ELI: The **Mishnah**, the earliest major written collection of **Rabbinic Jewish law and teaching**—a foundational record of the Oral Torah (the legal and interpretive tradition that accompanies the Written Torah), spells it out in compelling language. It says:

> Adam was created alone to teach you that one who destroys a single life is as if they destroyed an entire world; and one who saves a single life is as if they saved an entire world.
>
> —Mishnah Sanhedrin 4:5

Why? Because each person is a whole universe of possibilities—children, ideas, kindnesses, songs, tears—that now will never exist.

NIKKI: So the Torah is basically saying: "You're not just killing *this* person; you're killing all the worlds that would have come through them."

RABBI ELI: Exactly. And the same **Mishnah** adds another point: Adam was created alone so that no one could say, "My ancestors are greater than yours," and so that heretics would not say, "There are many rulers in Heaven."

So baked into the prohibition of murder are three deep ideas:

1. EVERY HUMAN IS INFINITELY VALUABLE.
2. NO HUMAN IS INHERENTLY "LESS THAN" ANOTHER.
3. THERE IS ONE GOD AND ONE HUMAN FAMILY.

You can hear how universal that is.

CAIN, ABEL, AND THE FIRST MURDER

NIKKI: And the first murder in the Torah is literally *between brothers*—Cain and Abel.

RABBI ELI: Genesis shows murder as a breakdown of the most intimate human bond. Cain kills his brother, and God says, *"Your brother's bloods cry out to Me from the ground"*—"bloods" in the plural. The commentaries say that it includes all his potential descendants.

So, from the very beginning, the Torah frames murder not as a technical crime but as **a wound in creation itself**. The earth soaks up the blood and "cries out." Reality itself is protesting.

Every soul is sent into the world with a **unique tikkun**—a specific repair or mission that only it can do. And from a mystical point of view, murder is not just "ending a life." It's like: **Silencing a once-in-history Divine melody.**

You're destroying the particular way God wanted to shine through *this* person, at *this* time, in *this* body. This has cosmic implications: A spark that was supposed to be elevated through this life has been violently interrupted.

NIKKI: So if I were to kill a person, I'm vandalising God's artwork?

RABBI ELI: The Torah gives the legal and ethical frame; Kabbalah gives you the cosmic drama behind it.

JUDAISM AND THE RADICAL SANCTITY OF LIFE

NIKKI: Everyone says life is sacred; where does Judaism put its particular emphasis?

RABBI ELI: **It's how far we're prepared to go to protect life, even at the cost of other mitzvot.**

The classic principle is **pikuach nefesh**—saving a life. The Talmud reads the verse *"You shall keep My statutes and laws that a person shall do and live by them"* to mean: **"live by them and not die by them."**

So we break Shabbat, eat on Yom Kippur, violate almost any commandment, if that's what it takes to save a life. The rabbis say explicitly that nearly all the mitzvot of the Torah are suspended for this. That's radical.

NIKKI: If someone collapses in synagogue on Yom Kippur, you call the ambulance, you drive them, you feed them—no hesitation?

RABBI ELI: Not only "you may," but "**you must.**" If a life is at stake, the rest is just commentary. And, this applies to every life.

Remember: The Noahide prohibition of murder comes from God's covenant with *all* humanity after the flood, and the Talmudic teaching about destroying or saving a single life is understood to include all lives.

Judaism does not have a single standard that makes only "our" lives sacred. The premise is that **all human life is a vessel for God's image.**

MURDER, SELF-DEFENCE, AND THE "RODEF"

NIKKI: But then what about self-defence? Or war? Judaism is clearly *not* pacifist.

RABBI ELI: Right, and this is another nuance.

The same tradition that says "Do not murder" also says: *"If someone is coming to kill you, get up early to kill him first."* That's from the Talmud, tractate Sanhedrin 72a, discussed in many later sources.

The person actively trying to kill is called a **rodef**—a pursuer. Jewish law says you must stop them, even with lethal force if there's no other option.

NIKKI: So the prohibition is not against *all* killing, it's against unjust killing.

RABBI ELI: Exactly. The point is:

- MURDER = *unjust* taking of a life, ignoring and defiling the image of God.
- SELF-DEFENCE = protecting your own image or that of another person.

And even here, **Halacha** (the comprehensive body of Jewish law derived from the Torah) tries to limit damage. Some authorities say you must, if possible, neutralise the attacker without killing them. Only if that's impossible does lethal force become permitted or required.

CAPITAL PUNISHMENT: A PRINCIPLE AND A DETERRENT

NIKKI: And how does this play into things like the death penalty? The Torah has capital punishment for murder.

RABBI ELI: It does—but here's where Judaism may surprise people.

On paper, the Torah lists death as the punishment for murder and a few other grave sins. But the Talmud then makes the **evidentiary standards so strict** that, in practice, executions were almost impossible.

The **Mishnah** famously says:

> A Sanhedrin that executes once in seven years is called a murderous court.
>
> —Talmud Makkot 7a

Rabbi Elazar ben Azariah says, "Even once in seventy years."

Rabbi Tarfon and Rabbi Akiva say, "If we had been on the Sanhedrin, no one would ever have been executed."

The death penalty here functions mainly as **a teaching tool**: It tells you how serious murder is. But the rabbis are terrified of killing even one person unjustly. Many later scholars conclude that capital punishment in Judaism is "more of a principle than a practice."

NIKKI: So Judaism says: Murder is so bad we *threaten* the worst punishment, then spend the rest of the teaching making sure we rarely use it.

RABBI ELI: Exactly. It's another way of saying: "Life belongs to God, not to us. Even when someone has desecrated that gift, we handle their life with trembling hands."

KABBALAH AGAIN: THE SOUL DOES NOT BELONG TO YOU

NIKKI: Come back with me to the Kabbalah for a second. You said earlier that each soul has a unique mission. How does that shape the way we think of killing—suicide, euthanasia, war casualties . . . all the hard stuff?

RABBI ELI: From the mystical perspective, your **soul is on loan.** It comes from a higher world, returns there after death, and in between, it is in your care for a specific journey of tikkun.

Here are the key points:

- Murder is grabbing what *isn't yours*—ending someone else's mission.
- Suicide is also a tragedy, because you're also taking what isn't yours—even your own life. Your body and your soul are on loan from God.
- Even in a just war, every casualty is seen as a great loss—each one is a Divine spark whose earthly chapter has been closed.

The basic posture is: **Life is unspeakably precious because it's Godly, and death is always heavy, even when justified.**

NIKKI: What does Jewish tradition say about euthanasia, assisted dying, or end-of-life? What about the difficult cases? People who are suffering from terminal illness, and our society says we can ensure dignity at the end of life?

RABBI ELI: It's delicate. In Judaism, life is sacred from beginning to end. We don't get to decide when a soul has finished its mission. Only God does.

At times we may be permitted to withhold *extraordinary* measures. But actively ending a life? That's not ours to do. And it's certainly not our place to judge the quality of life. Judaism insists that every life has value because it comes from God, not for any other reason.

There's an ancient story of a woman who saw a rabbi in agony. She dropped a pot to startle those praying for his recovery—and they paused. In that moment when they stopped praying, he passed peacefully. She didn't kill him. She let heaven decide.

So, we are opposed to euthanasia. But we do believe in dignity. In letting the soul return to God when its time comes.

NIKKI: That's profound. The idea that we hold space, but not control.

RABBI ELI: Exactly. Reverence means humility. It means we honour the soul's journey, even when it's painful.

THE THIRD LAW—A SNAPSHOT

NIKKI: So if you have to summarise . . . ?

RABBI ELI: I'd say Judaism is unusually legal and mystical at the same time. It says on the:

1. LEGAL SIDE:
   - It builds a detailed system—the Third and the Seventh Noahide Laws, the Ten Commandments, and homicide laws—around the sanctity of life.
   - It treats saving life as overriding almost the entire religious code.
2. MYSTICAL SIDE:
   - It sees each life as a unique manifestation of God's image expressed in human form.
   - Murder is thus not only a social crime but **a form of cosmic vandalism**—tearing a page out of a story God is writing through that person.

Put those together, and you get a powerful Jewish instinct: **Err on the side of life.**

DOING THE WORK—SOUL WORK

NIKKI: In the last section, we talked about "Do not murder" as this huge, cosmic thing—destroying a whole world, silencing a Divine melody. But most of us are (hopefully) not walking around with weapons. I am, however, wondering about murderous *thoughts*:

"I wish that person didn't exist."
"I'm done with humanity."
Or: *"I'm going to destroy them."*

Does wishing someone dead still sit under this Third Noahide Law?

RABBI ELI: In a very real sense, yes.

The Torah doesn't only say, "Don't kill." It also says:

You shall not hate your brother in your heart . . .
you shall not take vengeance, nor bear any grudge.

—Leviticus 19:17–18

You shall love the Lord your God with all your heart,
with all your soul, and with all your strength.

—Deuteronomy 6:5

So the commandment against murder is surrounded by laws about **hatred, revenge, grudges, and love.** The message is:

If you let hatred rot quietly in your heart, you're walking toward murder—even if you never lift a hand.

NIKKI: So "Do not murder" starts before I ever touch a knife.

RABBI ELI: And the Sages make that explicit.

The Talmud says: "One who embarrasses another in public—it is as if he sheds blood."

Spiritually speaking, humiliation is a kind of **soul murder**. The blood drains from their face; something in them collapses. So, yes: We're now in the territory of thought and speech murder—all the ways we quietly erase people in our minds and with our mouths.

KABBALAH: CONTROLLING THE "GARMENTS" BEFORE YOU KILL

NIKKI: How does Kabbalah help us with thought crimes? I'm thinking that once we're raging, our inner demons are well . . . pretty loud.

RABBI ELI: Kabbalah gives you a gentle but demanding answer:

You might not be able to control your impulses, but you can control your actions.

The Tanya teaches that the soul expresses itself through three "garments": **thought, speech, and action.**

You can't always stop a flash of hatred or a violent fantasy from popping up—that's the animal soul doing what it does. But you can decide:

- what thoughts you **feed your mind**,
- what words you **say out loud**,
- what actions you **take**.

Tanya calls the "intermediate person" (the *beinoni*) someone who may still *feel* ugly impulses, but refuses to let them into thought, speech, or action. And it insists: This level is **within reach of every person.**

NIKKI: So Judaism doesn't say "never have a dark thought." It says: "Don't dress it, don't feed it, don't let it out the front door."

RABBI ELI: Exactly. That's how we keep the third law in the modern world: We stop murder **upstream**—at the level of fantasies, grudges, and contempt.

Now, let's talk about some practices that train us to do that.

1. "Don't Hate in Your Heart": Honest Conversation as Anti-Murder

The Torah's first move against heart-murder is surprisingly practical.

> You shall not hate your brother in your heart.
> You shall surely rebuke your neighbor, and
> not bear sin because of him. You shall not
> take vengeance, nor bear any grudge.
>
> —Leviticus 19: 17–18

> You shall love the Lord your God with all your heart,
> with all your soul, and with all your strength.
>
> —Deuteronomy 6:5

In other words:

- Don't **stew in silent hatred.**
- If something is wrong, **talk** to the person.
- Don't **feed vengeance** or long-term grudges.
- **Aim for love**, not simmering resentment.

A core *practice* here is: **When I feel hatred rising, I choose either courageous, respectful conversation or a conscious internal release. Not a secret murder in my heart.**

NIKKI: So is withholding and refusing to talk about it honestly another form of violence?

RABBI ELI: It's the soil in which emotional murder grows. The Torah says: Hatred stored in the heart is spiritually dangerous. If I never speak, never clarify, never forgive—it curdles. This is the first step to wishing the other person erased.

2. Guarding Against "Blood-Words": No Humiliation Zones

NIKKI: And what about the really sharp things the TikTok world condones—sarcasm, shaming, the comment you *know* will land like a knife?

RABBI ELI: This is where the tradition is very stark.

The Talmud says: *One who publicly humiliates another forfeits his place in the World to Come."*

And the Zohar and later rabbis say that lashon hara "kills three" and that God will forgive many sins by repentance—except malicious speech against another.

So, a very concrete practice is: Declare specific spaces "no bloodshed zones" for speech.

For example:

- At your family dinner table, you make a quiet rule:
  We don't rip people apart here. No shaming. No character assassination.

- With friends and colleagues, you can gently say:
  Can we talk about ideas, and maybe avoid the personal?

Every time you **refuse** to join a pile-on or humiliate someone, you're keeping the third law with your tongue: You're *not* murdering a soul in front of you.

3. Love Your Fellow and See the Soul Before the Body

NIKKI: That's speech. What about the private thought level—when my inner monologue is basically a courtroom drama where I am judge, jury, and executioner?

RABBI ELI: Here, Kabbalah—and especially Tanya chapter 32—gives a powerful meditation.

The Tanya says all souls share a single root in the One God. Our bodies separate us; our souls are siblings.

So the practice is: Train yourself to see the soul first.

When someone triggers you, you silently remind yourself:

- "This person also has a soul seated in God's Oneness."
- "I'm seeing their *body-self* and behaviour; I'm not seeing their whole story, their pain, their Divine spark."

The Tanya actually says the **foundation of the whole Torah** is lifting the soul above the body—starting with how you look at other people.

NIKKI: So instead of mentally stabbing them, I try to see them as . . . malfunctioning light?

RABBI ELI: Kind of, but you may still need boundaries, justice, and consequences, while refusing the inner act of saying: "You are nothing. You shouldn't exist." That inner act is the seed of murder.

4. "Keep Your Tongue from Evil": Psalm 34 as a Daily Drill

RABBI ELI: There's a beautiful little "drill" hidden in Psalm 34. It asks:

> Who is the man who desires life . . . ?
> Keep your tongue from evil,
> and your lips from speaking deceit.
> Depart from evil and do good;
> seek peace and pursue it.

Notice the steps:

1. TONGUE WORK—stop using your mouth for harm.
2. BEHAVIOURAL WORK—turn from evil, do good.
3. RELATIONAL WORK—actively seek and chase peace.

A daily practice could be:

- In the morning or at night, say those verses slowly.
- Ask yourself three questions:

- "Did my tongue do violence today?"
- "Did I *choose* not to act when I could have done good?"
- "Did I escalate instead of seeking peace?"

That's a very beautiful way to keep the third law: not just "I didn't kill anyone," but "I tried to be a person who seeks peace and protects life with my mouth and my choices."

BRINGING IT ALL TOGETHER

NIKKI: So, Eli, you mentioned a lot of religious wisdoms around murder of the soul. Can you do a quick summary to save us flicking back through our conversation?

RABBI ELI: I like to think of it like a toolkit:

- **Leviticus 19** tells you: Don't hate in your heart; don't take revenge; talk it out; aim for love.
- **The Talmud and Zohar** warn: Humiliation and **lashon hara** are forms of killing; guard your tongue like a weapon.
- **Tanya** teaches: Your garments—thought, speech, and action—are always in your hands; you can choose not to clothe your soul in violence.
- **Tanya** also teaches: Focus on other people's sacred soul, not their possibly flawed behaviour.
- **Psalm 34** invites you, daily: Keep your tongue from evil, seek peace, pursue it.

NIKKI: So every time I choose not to humiliate, not to gossip, not to indulge in revenge fantasies, I'm not just "being nice"—I'm honouring a cosmic command: **Do not destroy a world.**

RABBI ELI: Exactly. You're treating every person—including yourself—as a Divine universe that God wanted here.

And that is how the Third Noahide Law isn't just a prohibition; it becomes a daily spiritual practice of **protecting life in thought, in word, and in deed.**

FINAL THOUGHTS ON THE SANCTITY OF HUMAN LIFE

NIKKI: If I'm an ordinary person reading this chapter on "Do not murder," and I already know I'm not going to shoot anyone . . . what's the takeaway?

RABBI ELI: Two thoughts:

FIRST: The Talmud extends the command not only to literal murder but to **indifference to danger**. If your negligence can easily cost someone their life—drunk driving, unsafe workplaces—you're flirting with this Law.

SECOND: We expand the meaning of murder beyond physical killing alone. Shaming someone publicly, driving them to despair, can be a kind of soul murder. The Law is about bodies, but the *spirit* of it is: Never treat any human being as expendable.

NIKKI: The Third Noahide Law is less "Don't be a murderer," and more "Live like every person you meet is a universe of light you are responsible for nurturing."

RABBI ELI: Exactly.

RABBI ELI: In our modern world of busyness, commitments, stress, and constant change, it asks us to stop and remember: Protect life in all its forms. Choose kindness over cruelty. Speak with care. Honour the image of God in every person. Resist hatred, even when it's trending on social media. Protect the vulnerable. And above all, remember: Every human soul is a universe. Let us never be the ones who extinguish it.

NIKKI: What's our task now, in this world that feels like it's unravelling?

RABBI ELI: The same as always.

Choose life.

Honour life.

Protect life.

Be a living example.

You don't need to save the whole world. Just one person. One soul. That's a universe.

Even a kind word. Even a prayer. Even a Shabbat dinner. These things are radical acts in a world addicted to violence. Every time you affirm life—with love, with dignity, with holiness—you fulfil this Law.

No murder, yes, of course.
But also: yes to life.
Yes to compassion.
Yes to reverence.
That's how we stay human.
That's how we stay Jewish.

A NOTE: Some people carry God in the way they walk through the world. They're not loud about it. They don't need to be. They have a gravity that pulls you back toward what really matters. Eli was like that—steady, courageous, unusually alive to the image of God in other people. He didn't just teach "Choose life." He made it feel like a daily, doable decision. It's heartbreaking that someone like him was taken. And it's more than personal grief—it's a loss to the whole moral ecosystem. The world needs more people like Eli: human beings so rooted in holiness that they become a compass for everyone around them. If, like me, you're wondering what we do now—this is part of it. We carry the teaching forward. We keep choosing life. For Eli, for God, and most importantly, for each other.

CHAPTER 4

Do Animals Have Souls?

NOAHIDE LAW 4: NO EATING FLESH FROM A LIVING ANIMAL

(Act Compassionately)

But you shall not eat flesh with
its life, that is, its blood.

GENESIS 9:4

ᔕ

THE ORIGINS OF THE FOURTH LAW: DO NOT EAT THE FLESH OF A LIVING ANIMAL

Of all the Seven Noahide Laws, this one may sound the most peculiar to modern ears—archaic and out of step with contemporary Western life: *Don't eat the flesh of a living animal.* Who would do that?

But once again, the Torah isn't just giving us dietary rules. It's teaching us about **compassion, self-restraint, and the spiritual obligation to treat all creation with dignity**.

This Law originates just after the great flood, when Noah and his family step out into a cleansed but cautious new world. God grants them permission to eat meat—something that had not been allowed before the flood.

> Every moving thing that lives shall be food for you . . .
> But you shall not eat flesh with its life, that is, its blood.
>
> —Genesis 9:3–4

This is the birth of the Fourth Noahide Law.

Rabbi Eli says, "In essence, God is saying: *'If you are going to take from creation, you must do so ethically.'* You may eat meat—but you may not cause **undue suffering**. You must not eat the limb of a living creature. The animal must be fully dead before you take its flesh."

At its core, this is a law of **boundaries**. A call to elevate our relationship with the natural world from domination to stewardship.

Rabbi Eli puts it this way: "**This law is not only about what's on your plate. It's about what's in your heart. It's about your capacity to restrain your appetite for the sake of another creature's pain.**"

In Jewish law, this value blossoms into the broader concept of *tza'ar ba'alei chayim*—the prohibition against causing unnecessary suffering to animals. It underpins everything from **Kosher slaughter** (which requires the animal's death be swift and painless) to the requirement to **feed your animals before you feed yourself**. It's why Torah law forbids us from overworking animals, trapping them cruelly, or killing them for sport.

"The Torah gave us dominion," Eli says, "but not entitlement."

In modern terms, this Noahide Law challenges us to reflect on our food systems. How do we treat animals raised for meat? What does it mean, spiritually, to take a life—even an animal's life—for our own use?

Judaism doesn't demand vegetarianism (though it allows it), but it **demands consciousness**. It demands gratitude. And it demands that we never lose sight of the fact that **life—all life—belongs first to God**.

This law also teaches something deeper: cruelty corrupts. The sages teach that a person who mistreats animals will ultimately mistreat people. A society that permits cruelty to the powerless is a society in decline.

While this commandment may seem primitive, it is, in fact, a **moral litmus test**, a question we're asked each time we consume: *Are you aware of the cost? Are you acting with mercy? Are you taking only what is necessary to take?*

In an age where factory farming, environmental degradation,

and disconnection from nature are rampant, this ancient law calls us back to something radically humane:

To eat with humility. To live with conscience. And to never let our hunger override our compassion.

A NOTE ON OUR CONVERSATION

Whilst Rabbi Eli was a maverick and an agent for change, he also recognised the value of preserving Jewish traditions. You'd be mistaken if you thought there was any blind adherence to outdated principles out of zealotry or religious superiority. Eli ate in a strictly Kosher way because he believed every moment in life, every action you take was an opportunity to connect with Hashem (God).

When I was first getting to know Eli, and I was still recovering from my *brush with death*, we set a date for him to come over and attach a mezuzah (a small handwritten parchment scroll with Hebrew verses from the Torah) to our front door. To prepare for this auspicious event, my mother and I drove an hour to a Kosher supermarket in the Eastern suburbs. We bought Kosher whiskey (he liked a splash of whiskey on special occasions) and Kosher honey cakes. I was quite proud of myself—mission accomplished. I zeroed in on Kosher delicacies and discovered something entirely new about my city and my culture.

On the day of the mezuzah ceremony, Rowan unboxed the

fancy whiskey, imported from Israel, and I served the cakes. Eli gulped down a shot of whiskey with relish, wished us l'chaim, but the cakes sat dully on the plate as we chatted over celebratory drinks. Our lives were outside the religious and social customs of observant Jewish rituals, and neither Rowan nor I realised that Eli couldn't eat the cakes because we didn't keep a Kosher kitchen. To this day, I don't know why the glass serving the whiskey was okay, but not the plate, the forks, or the cakes. Note to self: Ask a rabbi . . .

As a child who was brought up in a secular household with secular Jewish parents, I was challenged by my Jewish identity. I didn't want to stand out, as Eli did (as an out and proud Jew). I desperately wanted the opposite—to blend in.

When I was about ten years old, my German Jewish grandparents came to stay with us. I remember my mother and my grandmother arguing over how wild my brother, sister, and I were and how awful my parents were for neglecting our Jewish education. A week later, we were dispatched to Sunday school at the nearest synagogue. Mum and I fought about me going, but like most arguments I had with my mother, she won the battle, and I submitted . . . until I could regroup.

On the first day of Sunday school, they put my sister and me in one group and my brother, who was much younger, in another. The teacher, an earnest young scholar, went around the circle asking us what we ate for breakfast. Here was my chance—and I took it.

Proudly, defiantly, I said, "Eggs and bacon." A hushed silence quickly descended over the group. The teacher asked me if I knew that eating bacon was wrong according to Jewish law, and I gave a loud, rebellious "Yes!" in reply. I was sent from the room to the Chief Rabbi, and my parents were promptly called to remove us, lest I infect the others with my blatant disrespect.

We never went back to Sunday school.

Until I met Rabbi Eli, I had not thought about that story for decades. But his mindfulness about food started to nudge at the edges of my consciousness—something long buried—that Jewish adherence and observance weren't imposed as a punishment; they were simply a choice.

Eli made that choice every day because he saw God in a leaf, a stone, a lamb, and a human life. Eli saw, felt, and experienced God in a way that was mystical and cosmic, yet also grounded, human, and real. I'd never met anyone like him, and I never will again.

NIKKI: We're up to the Fourth Noahide Law. And I've been reading up about it. "No eating flesh from a living animal." On the face of it, it's . . . odd. Who does that?

[I see Eli's face light up because this is his favourite place—the spot where an ancient, seemingly strange law suddenly reveals an entire moral universe.]

RABBI ELI: It's interesting. One reason this was even a thing is that in the olden days, they didn't have refrigeration.

NIKKI: Right.

RABBI ELI: So, what they would actually do is cut off the meat limb by limb and keep the animal alive for as long as possible. I know it sounds crazy, but there was a lot of crazy stuff that happened back then. And this is what God implemented and decreed after the flood—that it should no longer happen.

NIKKI: It's horrifying and, at the same time, you can see the bleak logic of it. No fridge, no freezer, no ice. You want fresh meat, you . . . keep the animal fresh. Alive.

The only "living" thing I can think of today that people eat is an oyster. Because it's still alive when you swallow it. Everything else is dead by the time it gets to the plate. And even there, if you ate a *dead* oyster, you'd probably get poisoned. I can see there's so much common sense woven into the Kosher laws of food preparation—salting, removing the blood, and a whole bunch more.

RABBI ELI: But be careful not to mix up a universal law that applies to all of us, and Kosher law which is specific to Jews.

NIKKI: But we live in a world of very intensive farming: animals raised in cramped sheds just to be killed for food. Does this Law—no flesh from a living animal—have anything to say to that?

THE FOUR LAYERS OF CREATION

RABBI ELI: Okay. There are a couple of things to unpack. First, it's important to know that, according to Kabbalistic philosophy, there are four types of creations, and each one is a level beyond the other. Each one is there to serve the ones above it.

Let's start with the inanimate. Stones, earth—things that *seemingly* don't have life. And I say "seemingly" because they *do* have life. Everything has life, because everything is a manifestation of God, and because everything has life and God within it, everything needs to be respected.

NIKKI: Everything? Even rocks? Dirt?

RABBI ELI: Everything. But there are different levels of respect, corresponding to the level of Godly energy something contains. You don't have to respect dirt in the same way you respect a leaf on a tree. And you don't have to respect a leaf on a tree in the same way you respect an animal. And you don't respect an animal the same way you respect a human being.

The four levels are: the inanimate (like rocks and dirt); then what grows—produce, flowers, trees; then the one above that is animals; and the one above that is humans. In Hebrew, we have specific words for each of these (*domem* → *tzomeach* → *chai* → *medaber*). And humans are called *medaber*: "The one who speaks."

NIKKI: So the main difference between a human being and an animal is the power of speech?

RABBI ELI: The power of speech, which is a high level of intellect. Right?

Now, ultimately, according to Judaism and Kabbalah, all four of those elements are here to serve a higher purpose, which is Hashem—God. The inanimate is here to serve what grows; what grows is there to serve the animal; the animal is there to serve man; and man is here to serve God. It's a perfect cycle of creation.

It's man's job to take all four of those things and raise them back to their Source, by doing what? By revealing the spark of energy, the godliness, within all of them, and elevating it to God.

NIKKI: So even a carrot has a mission?

RABBI ELI: Absolutely. And an animal too. It's all to provide humans with the energy to serve God and do good in this world.

But this is not just the job of the Jew. It's the job of *every* human being: to respect the inanimate, to respect the environment, to respect produce, to respect the animal, and, of course, to respect fellow human beings. Ultimately, to serve Hashem.

As Jews, we're given a myriad of additional dietary laws to govern our lives, and by fulfilling this mission, the purpose is for the world to have a model. So that the world can learn from it and follow suit.

NIKKI: But the whole world doesn't have to keep Kosher?

RABBI ELI: No, not at all. Kosher is not one of the Noahide Laws. But the world *does* have to keep "no eating flesh from a living animal." The world *does* have to avoid cruelty. And the world does have to respect creation.

I tell my children, when you walk past a tree, you don't rip a leaf off the tree. That's a common thing kids do. You don't do it.

NIKKI: And you explain why?

RABBI ELI: I explain why. I don't just tell them off. I tell them: This tree is here for a purpose. Everything in this world is here for a purpose. It's not our job to destroy things needlessly. If it's for a useful purpose—okay.

ARE WE ALLOWED TO ENJOY FOOD IF IT COSTS A LIFE?

NIKKI: That's exactly what I wanted to ask. Food is one of our greatest sources of pleasure. We have desires, and food is one of the ways we sate them. Is it okay to relish your food, knowing it cost a life?

RABBI ELI: Pleasure is not a bad thing. God gave us pleasure. He gave us pleasure in many parts of our lives. Some people think that being religious or devout means removing all pleasures. That's more of a Catholic thing than a Jewish thing. You know, Catholic priests don't have wives, nuns don't have intercourse. Monasteries, asceticism . . .

But that's not the Jewish way. God wanted us to have enjoyment in life. In fact, how are we supposed to understand God's pleasures if we don't have pleasure ourselves?

NIKKI: I love that. We learn about Divine pleasure by feeling human pleasure.

RABBI ELI: Exactly. And pleasure is one of the things we have in life that's above our understanding. It's beyond intellect. That's important—to experience something where you say, "I actually love this person and I can't explain why." That's beyond understanding. And that's how God wants His relationship with us to be: We do things for Him beyond our comprehension.

It doesn't make sense to keep Kosher. It doesn't make sense to keep Shabbat when your job requires you to work on Saturday. But God isn't asking us, the Jewish people, to only do what makes sense. He wants us to go beyond our comprehension.

To be clear, pleasure is important. But there's needless pleasure, and there's pleasure that leads to negativity. There's nothing wrong with a nice juicy burger. But when you reach a point where you're full, and now you want *another* burger "just because"—that's already a problem.

NIKKI: That's when it tips over.

RABBI ELI: Yes. Because that can lead to obesity, it can lead to sexual arousal not in the right place, it can lead to abuse of Nature—like you said before, eating without any awareness that an animal lived and died for that meal.

NIKKI: So it goes beyond pleasure, into perversion.

RABBI ELI: Exactly. You couldn't have said it better. Overindulgence stops being pleasure. It turns into something else. It can turn into depression, addiction, and pain.

So again: Pleasure is not frowned upon. It's important. But it has to be framed.

And this is already connected to our topic. Because before God ever told humanity about Kosher, He drew a line: *No flesh from a living animal.* In other words, you are allowed to enjoy the meat; you are not allowed to detach your enjoyment from the basic dignity of the creature. You may not torture the animal to prolong your pleasure.

That was the first boundary.

SACRIFICES, ANIMAL SOULS, AND WHAT GOD REALLY WANTS

NIKKI: I have to say, I still struggle with the idea of sacrifices. The Torah describes God taking "pleasure" in sacrifices; I think it even says that the sacrifice emits a "pleasing aroma." Why would God enjoy an animal being killed and burnt?

RABBI ELI: As a modern person, growing up in a modern society, I struggled with that too. A lot. Why would God take pleasure in killing an animal? I was learning a discourse—a talk by the Rebbe, based on a discourse of the first Chabad Rebbe, the Alter

Rebbe, Rabbi Schneur Zalman of Liadi (1745–1812), the author of the Tanya, the core text for Chabad philosophy.

They offer a verse from the Torah about sacrifices.

The verse literally reads: "A person who will bring from you a sacrifice to God . . . you shall bring your sacrifice" (Leviticus 1:2). It repeats the word "sacrifice"—*korban*—twice. The Hebrew root of *korban* is *karov*, closeness.

You can read it like this: "A person who wants to come close to God—from you. From within you—*that* is the sacrifice you bring."

It's not just teaching us how to offer an animal on the altar. It's teaching us a timeless lesson: When we want to draw closer to God, we have to look inward at our own animal instincts and our own animal soul and sacrifice *them*.

NIKKI: I get it. The real sacrifice is my ego, my overindulgence, my inner "animal"?

RABBI ELI: Exactly. Our temptations, our overindulgence in pleasure—that's what we "offer." The more you remove your ego, the more room you make for Hashem in your life.

That's one point.

Another point, as we said earlier, is that the purpose of the animal is to serve man. Its mission is to be elevated by us. That's why, as a religious Jew, I'm never going to become vegan based on the idea that "killing animals is immoral." Medically? Maybe. But not morally. The Torah allows us—doesn't *force* us, but allows us—to slaughter animals for food and for sacrifices.

NIKKI: But then, where does compassion come in?

RABBI ELI: Now we get to the soul of the animal—literally. The soul of the animal is longing to be brought back to its Source, to God. And the way for that to happen is by us slaughtering the animal in the most humane way we can. Then using its meat and its life in the service of God—by eating it with a blessing, with gratitude, with moderation, by using its energy to do good, or by using it as a sacrifice in the Temple.

It's almost like the animal is waiting, just like the mango on the tree is waiting to be plucked, just like the soil is waiting for seeds to be fruitful and therefore to be elevated. We're doing it a favour by helping it fulfil its mission.

But here's the key: "No eating flesh from a living animal," says you may not fulfil your mission by *denying* the animal its basic dignity. You may not elevate it through cruelty.

HOW KOSHER SLAUGHTER TRIES TO BE HUMANE

NIKKI: So, would you say that Jewish slaughter, *shechita*, is actually designed to be the most humane way?

RABBI ELI: Yes. I'll tell you something interesting. Have you ever cut your finger on a very sharp knife?

NIKKI: Yes, of course.

RABBI ELI: If you cut yourself with a rough blade, it hurts a lot. But with an extremely sharp blade, sometimes you don't even notice until you look down and see the blood.

There are many intricate laws governing the knife. A *shochet*, a ritual slaughterer—my grandfather was one—is rarely a bloodthirsty brute. If you meet a *shochet*, they're usually the most refined people. They study Torah voraciously, and they pray and recite a blessing before slaughter. They regard it as a sacred task rather than a violent occupation.

They run their fingernail along the blade very gently. If they feel even the tiniest bump, the knife becomes non-Kosher. They're not allowed to use it.

NIKKI: That's extraordinary. I've never heard that in my life.

RABBI ELI: Most people haven't. And they carry special stones to sharpen the knife. They can't put the blade to the animal's throat until it's perfectly smooth.

There's also a lot of symbolism here. Kabbalistically, every one of us has an "animal soul." It wants to eat, sleep, have sexual relations, live comfortably. Normal things. And we also have a godly soul that wants connection, meaning, and transcendence.

In animals, the head and the backside are at the same level. In a human being, the head is above the heart. This is highly symbolic. Our minds are supposed to lead, not be dragged along by the physical body and desire. The heart isn't shut down—but it's educated, guided, disciplined.

Consuming "flesh from a living animal" represents a picture

of the opposite of what God wants from us: the human behaving like a beast, pure appetite without mind or mercy. Without soul. The Fourth Noahide Law says: This is *not* what you are.

DO ANIMALS AND HUMANS SHARE THE SAME KIND OF SOUL?

NIKKI: In Hinduism, for example, there's this idea that you might start as an ant and then, through karma and reincarnation, eventually become human. Is that a Jewish concept? Can a sheep become a human, or is a human always a human?

RABBI ELI: We're absolutely always human. And I'll take it even further: A baby is born in absolute purity. The peak of humanity is the perfection of that pure baby.

In life, we grow, we experience the world, we fall, we get up, we fall again. The word we use is *teshuva*—which means *return.*

NIKKI: Return to what?

RABBI ELI: Return to the purity you had when you were born. Where your soul was untainted. And deeper still: Return to God. Return to your own soul.

It doesn't mean dying. It's meant to happen *in* our lifetime. We can become pure again by constantly growing, studying, training ourselves to do what the mind knows is right, making sacrifices—but not extreme ones, for example ones that harm our body.

We have designated times of year when we fast, such as Yom Kippur. We don't eat or drink for twenty-five hours. It's a reminder of who we really are: a soul connected to Hashem, above the physical and animal needs for food and drink. Then we're meant to bring that awareness *back* into eating, into living.

God wants us to eat. He wants us to benefit from the world—but in a very organised and careful way—so that we can fulfil our mission: to elevate the whole world—physically and spiritually—so that all mankind can coexist together in the most beautiful form.

NIKKI: So the human soul is always human. The animal soul is always animal. They're not interchangeable.

RABBI ELI: If they were the same or interchangeable, I could transform into an animal. But I can't. As much as I might want to some days. We all acknowledge there is a life-force behind an animal and behind a human, but it's not the same type of energy.

BLOOD, THE SOUL, AND WHAT WE EAT

NIKKI: You mentioned before that there's a problem with eating the "soul" of the animal. Can you explain that?

RABBI ELI: For Jews, one of the main issues with eating non-Kosher animals is the blood. The Torah has a separate commandment for Jews not to eat blood. Because "the soul is in the blood."

The life-force of the body is carried in the circulation of the blood. What pushes that blood is the soul. The animal soul, or the soul of the being, is in the blood.

It's fundamental to understand that we're superior to the animal in terms of our mission. When we eat an animal, we raise the animal's soul directly into ours.

Let's break it down:

Nefesh vs. Neshamah

- **Animals** have a **nefesh ha'chiyunit / Nefesh HaBehemit**—an *animal soul*: instinct, emotion, movement, life-force.
- **Humans** have that **plus** a higher **neshamah**—a Divine, God-seeking soul capable of free moral choice and a conscious relationship with God.

So, when we say "we consume the animal's soul," we mean:

- We take in its **nefesh** (life-force/instinct), but not a full humanlike neshamah.
- That animal nefesh becomes **fuel** for our own *animal* and *Divine* souls:
    - If we harness it for mitzvot, learning, kindness, and prayer, it's **uplifted**.
    - If we harness it for greed, lust, and violence, it's **coarsened** and we become more **animalistic**.

Some Kabbalists go further and speak of actual **gilgulim**—human soul-sparks that can be temporarily stuck in animals, then released through proper handling and consumption. That's more esoteric, but it strengthens this theme: **Eating is a spiritual transaction with the soul of the animal.**

NIKKI: It's a funny thing, but I have noticed that some people who don't eat animals at all often seem quite spiritual—almost airy.

RABBI ELI: Correct. They're not engaging with the soul of the animal at all. For us, when we eat the permitted animals in the right way, it actually *enhances* our soul. It allows us to elevate that animal soul to God.

Judaism is constantly reminding us: There is a soul in this creature. Respect it. Don't turn your dinner into an act of desecration.

In summary, whether Jewish or not, the point is: Don't treat a creature as a living buffet. And more broadly—don't cause needless cruelty.

BLESSINGS, GRATITUDE, AND MINDFUL EATING

NIKKI: You used a word earlier that I keep coming back to: **reverence.** Do we have a gratitude prayer for food? Because if we do, I want it in the book right here, in this chapter, for everyone to use.

RABBI ELI: In Jewish tradition, every time we put something in our mouth, there's a blessing. A *beracha*. We say: "Blessed are You,

God our Lord, King of the universe . . ." and then, depending on what we're eating, we complete it differently.

If it's fruit from a tree we say, "Who created the fruit of the tree." If it's something that grows from the ground, we say, "Who created the fruit of the ground." For wine, which is special, "Who creates the fruit of the vine." For bread, there's a special blessing of "*Hamotzi lechem min ha'aretz*"—"Who brings bread out of the earth."

It does two things. First, it acknowledges that everything comes from the Creator. Second, it's like asking permission in awe.

Then, after we eat, there's an after-blessing—the *birkat ha-mazon* for bread, or shorter blessings for other foods. That's the "thank-you."

So before: "May I?" After: "Thank You."

NIKKI: And if you've got a whole plate—vegetables, meat, grains—do you say it for every item?

RABBI ELI: Yes. But when you eat bread at a meal, the blessing over the bread covers everything else. Bread is considered the most superior of the growing things, what we call produce. It's the staple food of humanity.

So, imagine if everyone took a moment before eating to simply say: "Thank You, God, for this food . . . and for the animal that gave its life." Imagine if that were our social norm. How different our factory farms would look.

THE FOUR STEPS TO MINDFUL EATING

A few thoughtful ways to eat by the grace of God, where every bite becomes a small act of prayer.

An exploration in four stages:

1. PAUSE AND PERMISSION—"This is not mine."
2. TASTE AND THANKS—"This is a gift."
3. INTENTION AND ELEVATION—"Let this become energy for good."
4. GRATITUDE AFTER—"I return this moment to its Source."

You can do the whole thing in under two minutes, or stretch it into a longer meditation.

1. Pause and Permission—Before the first bite

JEWISH ROOT: In Jewish law, eating without a *beracha* is compared to "stealing" from God. The blessing is how we "ask permission."

PRACTICE:

- Put the food in front of you, but **don't eat yet**.
- Take one gentle, conscious breath.
- Say, preferably out loud, even if quietly, the appropriate blessing (e.g., over bread):

Baruch atah Adonai, Eloheinu Melech ha'olam, hamotzi lechem min ha'aretz.

Blessed are You, God our Lord, Sovereign of the universe, Who brings forth bread from the earth.

- As you say it, let one simple thought rise:

This food is not "mine." It comes by the grace of God.

RABBI ELI: In that one breath between plate and mouth, the food stops being just "stuff I'm entitled to" and becomes "a gift I'm about to receive."

2. Taste and Thanks—The first three bites

JEWISH ROOT: Rabbi Eli speaks of Divine "sparks" in everything; we elevate them by using the fruits of the earth with awareness and for a higher purpose.

For the **first three bites**, slow everything down:

1. FIRST BITE—NOTICE THE MIRACLE.
   - Take a small bite.
   - As you chew, silently name **the steps it took to arrive here:** *Rain. Soil. Sun. Farmers. Hands that baked this.*

- Inner line:
  So many stories had to happen for this to reach my hand. And every one of them orchestrated by God for my benefit.

2. SECOND BITE—FEEL THE GRACE.
   - Take another bite.
   - Bring your mind to **the life that was given**—especially with animal products:
     A living soul, a nefesh chayah, gave its life so mine can continue.
   - Let a brief thank-you arise: "By God's grace I eat. By God's grace I live."

3. THIRD BITE—OFFER IT UPWARDS.
   - Take a third bite.
   - As you chew, set a very simple intention:
     May the energy from this food become strength for good—for kindness, for courage, for learning, for prayer.

You're quietly telling your own animal soul: This isn't just for comfort, this is fuel for my mission.

After those three bites, you can relax and eat normally—the "frame" has already been set.

3. Intention and Elevation—Once during the meal

Somewhere in the middle of the meal, pause for just a moment.

JEWISH ROOT: In Hebrew the word "*lishmah*"—which

means "for its own sake," refers to performing a commandment without selfish motives, but purely for the sake of God, the Torah itself, or the inherent connection to the Divine, embodying true, selfless intention and devotion. Eli suggested that eating to keep the body in healthy order to serve God is a form of lishmah, that it's a service to God to keep the body in healthy order.

PRACTICE:

- Put down your fork or bread for a few seconds.
- Let one sentence pass through your mind:

I am eating by the grace of God, and I want this food to become life and light in the world.

---

4. Gratitude After—Birkat Hamazon as integration

JEWISH ROOT: The Torah explicitly commands blessing *after* eating and being satisfied ("You shall eat and be satisfied and bless . . .")

If you want a simple, accessible close to the practice:

- When you finish, don't jump up immediately.
- Take one breath and say:

Blessed are You, God our Lord, Sovereign of the universe,
for the food and the grace with which You sustain me.

- Let yourself feel, even for a heartbeat: *"I did not earn this moment. It was given."*

PRAYER FOR BREAD

Blessed are You, God our Lord, King of the universe, who brings forth bread from the earth.

בָּרוּךְ אַתָּה יְ-יָ אֱלֹקֵינוּ מֶלֶךְ הָעוֹלָם, הַמּוֹצִיא לֶחֶם מִן הָאָרֶץ.

Baruch atah Adonai, Eloheinu Melech ha'olam, hamotzi lechem min ha'aretz.

WHAT ABOUT FACTORY FARMING AND INDUSTRIAL CRUELTY?

NIKKI: That brings us to the uglier part. As a society, given the challenges of feeding large populations, we've evolved toward industrial farming of plants and animals. And when you think about it, there's something corrupt about it. Mass cruelty. Battery hens with miserable lives. Feedlots. Machines, not farms.

I don't keep Kosher, so I often pause before I eat a piece of meat and try to give thanks for the animal that gave its life. But there's always this nagging sense of horror. My daughter feels it too. She went through phases of worrying about the souls of the animals on her plate and contributing to grotesque farming practices. She'd regularly ask, "Mum, should I be a vegetarian?" Because she's seen the footage on social media.

How does all of that sit with the Fourth Noahide Law? Is breeding animals for food, en masse, a problem?

RABBI ELI: Any level of animal cruelty is forbidden. That's also part of the Noahide framework. "No eating flesh from a living animal" is the headline, but the Sages understand it to include avoiding needless pain to animals.

Now, I'm not saying cruelty never happens in Kosher butcher shops. It probably does, sadly. But in my humble opinion, it should be called out for what it is. If a butcher is cruel, he should lose his Kosher certification.

Whether animals can be bred for food—*that* is not the problem. They can, as long as it's done with dignity, where the animal enjoys its life, where it doesn't feel constantly abused.

NIKKI: But how do we know if an animal "feels" abused or wronged?

RABBI ELI: A person who is doing wrong knows they're doing wrong. Deep down, they know. We don't need to overphilosophise it. If you look at a battery hen shed and your gut twists, you know.

That's where governments come in. Note that the last of the

Seven Noahide Laws is to establish courts of justice. So, when there's injustice—especially with one of the Noahide principles like animal cruelty—it's meant to reach the courts, the government, and be stopped.

The Fourth Noahide Law, as one of the guiding principles to establishing a new society, was the first step out of barbarism. Today, the same principle should push us out of industrialised barbarism. It's the same idea: *Don't prolong your pleasure by prolonging another creature's pain.*

HOW A SINGLE LAW CAN HELP HEAL A CHAOTIC WORLD

NIKKI: There's something almost absurd about it, in a beautiful way. Out of all the things God could have said to a violent, post-flood humanity, He says: "Don't eat flesh from a living animal." Why state something that should be obvious?

RABBI ELI: Because it's the most basic test of whether you see yourself as a human being or as a sophisticated predator. It's the line between appetite and morality. And between barbarism and civilisation.

You could say the first step in recognising that animals have a soul—however different from ours—is to stop eating them while they're still aware and suffering. The second step is gratitude and blessing. The third step is elevating them through mindful use.

NIKKI: It makes me think of what you once said about Jews being a metaphorical *shofar*—a trumpet call to the nations.

RABBI ELI: Yes. Chabad rabbis around the world are waking up to this. There's a lot of discussion among us about how to share the Seven Noahide Laws. The Rebbe taught that to prepare the world for the ultimate state of peace—the coming of Mashiach—the whole world has to know about God and about these universal laws.

Rabbis used to say: "We'll work on the Jews, let the world do what it wants." But that's not enough anymore. That's not my mission and that was not the Rebbe's mission.

A Jew is like a shofar. When you sound a shofar in the street, people don't get to choose whether they hear it. They hear it. In the same way, whether we like it or not, the world is listening to us.

NIKKI: Especially now. We're in the news every day, though not in a good way and not for the right reasons. Only a couple of years ago, we were like little turtles with our heads down. Now, people who never thought about Jews in their lives suddenly have opinions about us.

> A NOTE: It is brutally and gut-wrenchingly ironic now that Eli was literally killed, and that just weeks before we were having *this* conversation. I battled with myself about whether or not to leave this section in the book, but seeing this text comes from our actual conversations, and we were very aware that something awful was coming to the Jewish world, in this light, it's important to know that Eli and I were both thinking about how dangerous antisemitism had become.

RABBI ELI: A lot of those *opinions* are based on a corrupted version of who we are and what the Torah says. So, we have to step up. Each in our own way. You through writing. I through teaching.

And one of the simplest, most powerful ideas we can share is exactly this law you're writing about, which essentially boils down to one thing—respect for life. Recognition that even an animal—even a leaf—has a purpose and a spark.

TWO LITTLE SOULS AT A FRIDAY-NIGHT TABLE

As we begin to wrap up the call, I tell Eli something I've been wanting him to know.

NIKKI: Just before you go, I want to thank you for what you did with [my nephews] Joe and Levi on Friday night. [We'd been invited to the Chabad in Bondi to celebrate a special Shabbat dinner.] They've never had any real contact with their religion. It was significant for them—especially Joe. He's seeking his Jewish identity. I don't know where that will go. But you lit a spark in him. Now he knows there is a place for him that is beautiful and safe and welcoming. Two little Jewish souls were lit up on Friday night at your table, and I'm so grateful.

RABBI ELI: Amazing. Baruch Hashem. Thank God.

A NOTE: This encapsulates everything Rabbi Eli did for the world. He was a beacon for others to follow. He wanted to ignite his soul and nudge it gently into remembrance and connection. Joe was bereft when he heard about Eli's death. He made a pilgrimage across town, took flowers, and laid them at the memorial at Bondi, as so many thousands did, not knowing that Jews don't traditionally take flowers to a memorial—we take stones. But the truly grim thing is that just as Joe's Jewishness was awakening, he lost his natural guide and mentor. For Eli, if he were looking down on us from above, I suspect that, aside from leaving his beloved family, this would have been the tragedy of all tragedies: being prevented from continuing his work as a soul-deliverer and a light-activator. Immersed in the stream of love he channelled so effortlessly from his Creator, he had a seemingly infinite and super-human ability to give to others—especially when they needed him most—in hospitals, prisons, nursing homes, and even on the street. His assistant, Evie, told me that he once saw a Muslim man in the parking lot of a local supermarket and he went up to the man, with all his Eli-enthusiasm and almost childlike optimism, and asked him if they could join forces to bring light and healing to the world. "He simply didn't see anything strange about that," she said. His loss ripples through time and through the hearts left on earth without him to guide us.

ᔕ

We say our goodbyes. After we hang up, I sit for a long time before I move.

I think about souls—human, animal, inanimate. I think about my daughter agonising over a chicken schnitzel, about the faceless cows in feedlots, about the fact that my own life was once hanging by a thread in an ICU while Eli blew a shofar at my bedside to call my soul back.

Now, in the uncanniest way, I am charged with Eli's mission to bring light to the world. He switched roles on me. He was supposed to be the teacher, not me. How did that happen? I'm left with more questions than answers and no rabbi to offer me truth, solace, and wisdom.

So, do animals have souls?

Yes. Not like ours. Not made to speak, to choose, to do *teshuva*. But each creature carries a life-force that comes from the same Creator. And the Fourth Noahide Law plants a flag in the middle of history and says:

You may eat.
You may enjoy.
You may benefit from the world.
But you may *not* forget that everything you touch—stone, leaf, lamb, your own beating heart—was made by God for a purpose, carries a spark, and cries out to be treated with reverence.
You may not eat flesh from a living animal.
Because you are not an animal.
You are a human being.
And that difference—painfully, beautifully—matters.

CHAPTER 5

Is Stealing Really *That* Bad?

NOAHIDE LAW 5:
DO NOT STEAL
(Live Honestly)

You shall not steal, nor deal falsely, nor lie to one another . . . You shall not cheat your neighbour, nor rob him. The wages of him who is hired shall not remain with you all night until morning.

LEVITICUS 19:11, 13

ග

THE ORIGINS OF THE FIFTH LAW: DO NOT STEAL

It sounds simple, doesn't it? *Don't steal.* But in Judaism, this commandment is anything but basic. The prohibition against theft is a moral pillar that reaches far beyond pickpocketing or burglary. In Jewish tradition, to steal is not only to take something that isn't yours—it's to *undermine the entire foundation of trust that makes human society possible.*

This Noahide Law has its roots, like many others, in the story of **pre-flood humanity**. The Torah tells us:

> The earth also was corrupt before God,
> and the earth was filled with violence.
>
> —Genesis 6:11

Rashi (Rabbi Shlomo Yitzchaki, 1040–1105), the great French medieval commentator, explains that "violence" here refers specifically to *theft*. Not grand heists necessarily, but petty, systemic dishonesty—people taking what isn't theirs, ignoring boundaries, eroding mutual respect. In fact, the Talmud suggests that it was this kind of social corruption—not murder or idolatry—that sealed the fate of the flood generation.

Why?

Because when theft becomes common, no one feels safe. Because when people no longer respect the boundaries of *mine* and *yours*, all other values begin to unravel.

In the Torah, the commandment *"Do not steal"* appears explicitly in the Ten Commandments (Exodus 20:13) and is expanded throughout Jewish law to include:

- Theft of physical property
- Fraud, deception, and dishonest business practices
- Withholding wages
- Kidnapping (which, in Torah law, is the most severe form of "stealing"—the theft of a person)
- Even subtle coercion or pressure that deprives another of what is rightfully theirs

The deeper idea? **Ownership is sacred.** And not just because we're entitled to our things, but because God is the true Source of everything—and to steal is to break trust with both man *and* God.

As Rabbi Eli puts it: *"Stealing isn't just a crime. It's a spiritual betrayal. You're saying: 'I don't believe there's a system bigger than me. I don't believe I'm accountable to anyone. I take what I want because I don't believe there's a Supreme Judge watching.'"*

In today's world, theft doesn't always look like breaking into someone's home. It might look like pirating content online. Using someone else's work without credit. Taking credit for an idea that wasn't yours. Charging more than something is worth. Withholding payment to contractors. Dodging taxes. Cutting in line.

"There's even such a thing as stealing time," Rabbi Eli added. "Or stealing someone's reputation. Stealing trust. That's why Judaism has such strong teachings around *honest weights and measures*. Because if we can't trust the scale in the marketplace, how can we trust each other?"

The Jewish understanding of this law is radical in its depth: It tells us that **trust is the true currency of a moral society.** You can't legislate trust—you live it, person to person, moment to moment. And every time you take what isn't yours—whether it's money, time, honour, or credit—you chip away at the fragile social contract we all rely on to keep ourselves connected, not only to each other but also to God.

And just like the flood generation, when a society begins to normalise theft—in business, in politics, in daily life—the water rises, and society drowns.

To live by this law is to live with integrity. It's to recognise that the boundaries between people—their rights, their dignity, their property—are not obstacles. They are **sacred contracts** that help us live together in peace.

NOTES ON OUR CONVERSATION

When people are steeped in God, and this applies to any religion or spiritual belief system, they see the miraculous everywhere. For Eli, miracles weren't abstract; they were real, and they revealed

God's majesty and mystery. For this chapter, he told me a story that resonated with me personally because of my own miracle recovery and how synchronicity, signs, and symbols (that to many may appear random and meaningless) signify God's presence in our lives to people of faith.

That's something Rabbi Eli and I had in common. We both believed in miracles and their transformative power. You might be wondering what this has to do with the Fifth Noahide Law, "Do not steal," but it has everything to do with it. According to Eli, all the laws are essentially one law, wearing different garments, but with the same inner truth—one God commands us, one God calls us to see Him in his many facets, and one God shows up for us in a myriad of ways because He loves us so much that he wants us to experience him, in his infinite expressions, personally and profoundly.

As I write, I can't get the idea out of my head that Eli's life was stolen. It also makes me wonder whether Eli would view the shortness of his life as theft. I suspect, if he were here now, counselling me in my grief, he'd simply say, "It was God's will."

In his painful absence, I can but wonder . . .

Rabbi Eli Schlanger was the Jewish chaplain for the New South Wales Corrective Services. He drove all over the state to minister, sometimes just to one prisoner. Eli recounted a story where he'd recently attended a sentencing hearing for a Jewish prisoner who'd been making threats to the Federal Court. Eli attended court that morning with the prisoner's ninety-four-year-old mother, who was distraught.

"The man was clinically unwell. He didn't hurt anyone, but he'd made serious public threats, and although he had neither the means nor ability to carry out his threats, the police locked him up because he was being a menace.

"The judge entered the courtroom, sat down, and began, 'I would like to declare that I should recuse myself from this matter. I know this woman' (referring to the prisoner's mother). The judge, who was Jewish, knew the prisoner's mother from volunteering at the same charity.

"To our surprise, the Prosecutor told the judge that she didn't need to recuse herself, and the matter continued. The prisoner had already been detained for seven months, which the judge deemed sufficient punishment for the crime. The judge looked at me, a rabbi sitting next to the mother, and asked whether I'd been ministering to him, to which I nodded in assent. A minute or so later, the judge delivered her verdict and said the prisoner could be released as long as he stayed on his meds and continued spiritual study with me."

Eli calculated it like this: What were the chances that a judge would attend a matter involving a woman she knew and respected from their charity work together, on the same day that Eli was sitting in court in his role as spiritual guide and mentor to the prisoner?

No doubt about it, to Eli this was indeed a miracle.

On the day of our conversation about stealing, Eli had just picked up the prisoner from jail. "It just shows that if you show up for people in a time of need, you can make an impact," he said.

Eli had infinite energy for doing good. He told me often that when he visited prisoners, he didn't ask them about their crimes; it didn't matter to him. He was never afraid of them; he just wanted to be present to them and allow a conversation, like the ones we had, to unfold.

There were not many men like Eli in the world, which is why when his light went out, it was as catastrophic as a black hole consuming a star. I can only hope that through his words here, his wisdom and presence can endure beyond the short span of his human life.

THE ONE-DOLLAR TEST: WHY GOD CALCULATES IN ABSOLUTES, NOT FRACTIONS

I didn't think chapter 5 on "Do not steal" would begin with a pair of one-dollar socks. But that's where Eli wanted to start. Not with high finance or Wall Street or ancient tropes about Jewish usury. But with Kmart. A stroller. Three small kids. And a father who is tired, hungry, and just wants to get them home.

RABBI ELI: I might have told you the story before, but it's a lesson for life.

NIKKI: Go for it. I want to hear the story.

RABBI ELI: Many years ago, we went on a family holiday with a few friends to the Gold Coast. One afternoon, we went to Kmart with all the kids. We had a stroller with us, maybe three kids, it was winter, getting dark early, everyone was tired.

As we left Kmart, I noticed a pair of one-dollar socks on the stroller. And my first instinct—honestly, I was so irritated; I was such a controlling parent back then—was to make sure bedtime was on time, bath at six thirty, all of that. Today it's like, whatever, but then it was a big deal.

I'm standing there with these one-dollar socks on the stroller, and in my head, I'm going, "To hell with it, it's just one dollar." And then, within a split second, I said to myself, "Eli, it may be one dollar, but it ain't your one dollar."

NIKKI: You've painted a vivid picture, I can almost see you in the car park—the dark, the whining kids, the trolley, the ridiculous socks, and that quiet, inconvenient sentence landing in your mind like a pebble dropping into water.

RABBI ELI: Yeah! Right! So I turned around. I took the socks back into Kmart.

NIKKI: Of course you did!

RABBI ELI: After all that, I returned, and we've finally got to the car, I put the stroller in the car, the kids in the car, I get into the driver's seat, and my wife says to me, "Where's my wallet?"

I said, "I don't know . . . where is your wallet?"

She says, "I left it in the stroller."

I say, "I'm sure it's there."

She says, "Could you check?"

I get out—this is all a delay, the kids are grumpy, it's dark, the

Airbnb is twenty minutes away—and I go back to the boot. I search the stroller. No wallet. I search around the car. Nothing.

I go back to the mall, and I ask the security guard. I ask at the Kmart counter. Nobody's seen the wallet. Gone. Disappeared. Vanished.

I get back in the car. Deep breath. And I say, "It's all from Hashem. It's okay." At the time, every dollar mattered. We literally brought a few hundred dollars in cash for the trip, which was in Chaya's wallet, along with our credit cards. Losing that wallet was a big deal.

NIKKI: I get it, that kind of loss, it's not abstract. It hits the stomach.

RABBI ELI: Exactly. I said to Chaya, "It's all from Hashem. It's okay." We went back to the apartment, blocked the cards. And there's a Jewish concept called *kapparah*—atonement. When something like this happens, you say, "This is atonement for something. Thank God it's this and nothing bigger."

My wife is upset—nobody likes losing things. She feels this weight on her chest. Later, I'm cooking dinner with my brother-in-law, and Chaya suddenly jumps up from the couch, runs into the kitchen, and says, "Eli . . . my wedding rings were in my wallet."

NIKKI: Oh no.

RABBI ELI: I take another deep breath, and I repeat, "It's from Hashem. It's okay." I did a quick calculation in my head of what those rings were worth. A few thousand dollars. And I said, "It's just money."

She says, "Nope," and she's very agitated. I couldn't really deal with it. I called my father-in-law.

I say, "Shver, this is the story. Please can you talk to your daughter?"

He tells her about a famous sage, Rabbi Meir Baal Ha-Nes—there's this special charity box we have connected with his name. It's one of these Jewish "tricks": Whenever you lose something, you put money into this box, and you say, "Eloka d'Meir, Aneina—the God of Rabbi Meir, please respond to me." And nine out of ten times, you'll find your item.

She tells her father, "I don't have access to that box, and I don't have any money."

So, he says, "I'll do it for you. I'll be your emissary."

Great. I think, "There's nothing more we can do."

But she gets off the phone, turns to me, and says, "Nah. I'm not comfortable with this. Please go back?"

Not wanting to upset her further, I said, "Fine." My brother-in-law and I get into the car—again. I'm tired. I'm annoyed. I drive back to the mall. It's pitch-black. I'm rummaging through garbage bins, thinking maybe somebody took the money and threw the rest out. I ask a ranger in the park. I ask everyone. Nothing.

We return to the car. Defeated. Then my brother-in-law says, "Hey, look on the left, there's a Chinese light festival over there. Why don't you go to the booth and ask?"

I'm like, "Really?"

He says, "Yeah."

I get out and walk over. There's a girl behind the booth. She looks at me and goes, "Eli?"

I'm like, "Whaaaaaat?"

She says, "I messaged your wife on Facebook. I found her wallet. She didn't respond, so I messaged you. But if you're not Friends you don't get the notification . . ."

Long story short, she hands me the wallet. I open it. Everything is there. The cards. The cash. The rings.

I take out a hundred dollars and say, "This is for you."

And she bursts out crying.

She says, "I can't, I can't take it."

I say, "You're doing me a favour. Please. This is so important to my wife right now. Please take it."

She was thanking me. She says, "Wow, I can really do with it." And she takes it.

Her name was Lauren. I wrote to her years later to thank her for her honesty: "We'll never forget what you did for us." She wrote back, "Karma is real. I, too, have been blessed by the beauty of humanity many times."

The moral of the story? I was tested over one dollar.

Often, we think that if it doesn't bother anyone, if it doesn't harm anyone, if no one will know, we don't take it seriously. But we don't stop ourselves from stealing because we'll get into trouble, or we'll get caught, or we break a law of the land . . . That's not the deepest reason.

We don't steal because God said so.

And if God said so, there's no difference between a dollar and a million dollars. Because stealing . . . is stealing.

STEALING IN AN AGE OF "NO ONE WILL NOTICE"

NIKKI: In this context of "Because God says so," stealing is so much more. Obviously, "Do not steal" keeps a society on track, but these days, stealing can be so broad. It can be stealing someone's identity. Stealing someone's joy. Gaslighting. Stealing emotionally. Or, like you say, even an apple when you can't be bothered to weigh it properly at the supermarket is still stealing.

And I confess, I've done that. I've gone, "I didn't mean to have that bag of beans in my trolley, but I'm not walking back." And that *is* stealing.

As we're talking about it, I know that on the deepest level, that muddies your soul. It feels bad. It goes against our moral backbone, it's how to keep a cohesive society. This is the very essence of the Fifth Noahide Law: Don't take something that isn't yours, on any level, right?

RABBI ELI: Correct.

There's actually a preventative way of becoming someone who doesn't play games with theft, even with "little" things. There is a general rule in Judaism: To prevent ourselves from committing a sin, we do the complete opposite, by becoming a **giver** rather than a **taker**. That's the commandment to donate a tithe of our earnings.

This is the heart of the Noahide Law of "no theft." It's not only "don't take." It's an invitation to shape your entire character away from grasping, toward generosity. To live as someone who asks: *Where can I give? Who can I help?*

Remember back to the ICU after I'd said prayers for your recovery, when I asked your husband and daughter to give the gift of a single coin each day? That small mitzvah (**tzedakah**—righteousness or justice) is spiritually significant. The idea behind it is that the repetition of giving trains the person to make generosity part of their character, part of who they are. And there's a resonance in heaven too: The Talmud teaches that "charity saves from death," so we pray that in their giving, it echoes in God's realm. It creates merit. It creates humility, and it creates character.

NIKKI: Well, it worked. I survived. I am grateful to you for teaching my family this principle of tzedakah. As the recipient of that "charity" I feel the onus is on me now to give back.

FROM TAKING TO GIVING: THE PIT STORY

RABBI ELI: I recently heard a story, a beautiful parable.

There was a very wealthy man who fell into a pit and couldn't get out. Many people came along and said to him, "Let me help you, give me your hand." And he refused to take any help. He was so arrogant, he didn't want to accept help from anyone—even if it meant getting him out of the hole he was in.

Then a rabbi came along, whispered something to him, they locked hands, and the rabbi pulled him out.

The men around them asked, "Rabbi, what did you say?"

He said, "You all said, give me your hand. I said, take my hand."

He was happy to take, but he couldn't handle the word "give" or the idea of giving.

It's a beautiful idea. A person comes into this world to be a **giver, not a taker.** You *can* receive—that's different from taking. Receiving is a humbler version of taking.

NIKKI: That's a great illustration. I love that.

THE OBLIGATION OF GIVING: TRAINING THE SOUL NOT TO STEAL

NIKKI: I didn't know it was a rule, a commandment, to tithe your income. How much? How do you do it? What's the rule?

RABBI ELI: It's like this: 10 percent of your net income goes to charity. And there are laws about how charity works. As the saying goes, charity starts at home. We have an obligation to take care of our family first, then our local community; if we still have money left over, we support broader community and global charities.

NIKKI: Which makes sense. You look after family, then community, and then extend your reach when resources are available.

RABBI ELI: And there's a well-known thing about Jews—if you take all the hate off the internet and listen to people who actually appreciate the way Jewish communities build wealth, they'll describe something like this:

This is a real story. Take the Hasidic community in Melbourne, the one whose synagogue was firebombed. Generally speaking, Hasidic Jews are known for exactly what their name implies; *chassid* comes from *chesed*—kindness.

I was talking to one of them and asked, "You're quite an insular community. How do you do it? Without all the secular knowledge, how do you build wealth?"

He said, "It's very simple."

"When a young boy and girl get married—at eighteen, nineteen, twenty years old—they're approached by a family friend or an uncle. These are big families—ten kids each. And the uncle says, 'Listen, we've got a factory. We need toilet paper. This is where we normally buy it. We're going to give you the supplier's contact. You're going to buy from them, add 1 or 2 percent, and we're going to buy from you. And we'll introduce you to our friends. You'll be the toilet paper supplier to the community.' "

And this is how they build wealth. This is how they build up the next generation.

NIKKI: Amazing.

RABBI ELI: And you might ask, "Why would someone hand over their supplier, and on top of that be willing to pay extra?" Because in Judaism, the word for "charity" is *tzedakah*. *Tzedakah* means two things: **justice** and **righteousness**. Giving to the needy and deserving is not merely generosity or philanthropy; it's the fulfilment of a Divine commandment that fairness and justice form the basis of a civilised society. And remembering that nothing in this world *belongs* to us, it ultimately belongs to God.

That's how we keep a just world: by being givers, by looking for people we can help. That is also the channel through which God provides us with our own sustenance.

NIKKI: You can hear the flip side of "Do not steal" in that: *Do not clench your fist.* Live open-handed.

RABBI ELI: I started giving a tithe, properly calculated, seriously, maybe twelve years ago. At the time, I had a lot of credit card debt I couldn't get out of. For ten years, I had tried. I can't explain how, but within twelve months of starting to give a tithe, that debt cleared to zero.

And I haven't looked back since. I don't have credit card debt. I don't have a mortgage because I don't own a home, but since then, I have never been in a situation where I didn't have money for whatever our family needed. Somehow those extra car problems and doctor visits disappeared.

There is no question: God decides who will be rich, regular, or poor. It's not in my hands. If God wants me rich, He'll find a way. It's not like I sit on my tuchus [bottom] and do nothing; I work hard. But where I am financially is where God wants me, and I'm happy with that. Of course, I want more. Why? Because it allows me to give more.

And my kids—if they do a job, they give 10 percent from a

young age. From three, four years old. They make five dollars, fifty cents goes to charity. It's built in.

In the Torah, where it says you should give a tithe—*aser t'aser*—the word "*eser*" (ten) is written twice. The law is: minimum ten, maximum twenty. You're not allowed to give away more than 20 percent of your income.

But the Talmud notes something beautiful: *eser* (ten) has the same Hebrew letters as *ashir* (rich). By giving ten, you become *ashir*—wealthy.

And I consciously share stories with my kids. Once, I was at my wits end yet again, and called someone to help me send my daughter overseas to study. We didn't have much money at the time. He said, "It's not something I normally do, but you know what, Eli? Here's the money."

I didn't know it when I asked, but he broke himself to give that.

Then, he called me at the end of the day when the markets closed and said, "Eli, I don't know how to explain this, but I made ten times what I gave you today."

The promise is that if you give 10 percent, you get ten times back. There are books full of these stories.

JEWS, MONEY, AND THE STEREOTYPE OF DISHONESTY

NIKKI: Of course, in a chapter about stealing, we can't not talk about Jewish stereotypes. You can see why the outside world gives

Jews so much heat about money. Historically, in many countries, the only job Jews were allowed was moneylending; in many respects, Jews built the Western banking system. But still today, we're victims of terrible PR—that we control the whole world, the financial systems, that we're dishonest with money.

There is a grain of truth in the sense of visibility; we do punch above our weight in finance, Hollywood, and so on. But the stereotype is that we're crooks. This is pure misinformation.

So, how do we, as modern Jews, deal with the misinformation, and also deal with the true story underneath—that we tithe, we support each other? That threatens a lot of people.

RABBI ELI: First things first: We have a law in the Torah: *Dina d'malchuta dina*—the law of the land is the law.

Recently, I had a meeting with the local member of Parliament. She came with her aide, and one of the things she asked was about my chaplaincy for Corrective Services.

She asked, "How many Jews are there in prison?"

When I pulled out the number—anywhere between seven and nine—she waited for the word "hundred" to follow. Something big.

They looked at each other, shocked.

Then she turned to her aide and said, "Actually, that's not so shocking. Jews are very law-abiding citizens."

Of course, there are bad apples, but generally speaking, in a democratic society there is usually zero conflict between the local law and Jewish law. In fact, much local law stems from Judaism. We are upstanding citizens.

There's a caveat: unless local law directly prohibits a Jew from keeping the Torah. Soviet Russia, for example, banned circumcision and Jewish marriage, laws specifically against Jews. That's different.

What's hard for the world to understand is that Jews are generally law-abiding citizens and *still* manage to maintain a community that is different, tightly knit, and family-like.

They don't realise we see each other as family. If I expected you to be as close to me as you are to your brother or cousin, that would be ridiculous. But Jews really do see each other as one big family.

And there's another side—we're a little paranoid about being attacked. History reveals that. So we do need to stick together as a family.

Historically, when a country had a Jewish community, it flourished. Not because we're witches pulling strings, but because Jews are law-abiding, community-building, giving citizens. It's literally part of our DNA and a key religious command. When we enhance our own communities, we enhance the wider economy.

Here's the core of it: We believe in God, and God has instructed us how to live. We keep these laws because God said so, and we believe that brings blessing into the world.

The blessing isn't there because we're special; it's because we're keeping this special law.

STEALING IN A WORLD OF MORAL FLEX

NIKKI: For a long time, I thought of "no theft" as a simple command: Don't pinch someone's bike. Don't rob a bank. Now it feels much more slippery. In this crazy world, where very few people are tethered to the basic tenets of religion—Jewish or non-Jewish—people can easily justify stealing. They dilute it. "Oh, I accidentally stole that bag of beans, who cares?" Or more extreme things, like stealing someone else's husband or wife or fiddling their taxes. There's so much moral flex. I think we've stopped valuing things—because everything is disposable—but also stopped valuing *our own values.* In everyday terms, how do we deconstruct that? How do we help people realise that "no theft" is not just about crime, but about their own soul?

RABBI ELI: This is what this book boils down to: *Our morals are not our morals. They are God's morals.* The very first of the Seven Noahide Laws is to believe in one God. Everything in this world is God's, governed and watched by God. We're accountable to Him.

It's true that a person is not strong enough to build their own set of morals. Anyone who says they can do it on their own without rules and guardrails is lying.

I don't even blame them. We live in a permissive age. And we all have an animalistic soul with basic animal instincts. Animals desire and go after what feels good, tastes good. We have the same characteristics—unless they're tamed by just laws and rules.

The point is, we have to govern our lives by a higher power, something beyond us. That's a challenge, something to be conscious of daily. That's why Jews aim to bless God at least a hundred times a day. It's a reminder. Not because we're so righteous and close to God; it's the opposite. We remind ourselves constantly: There is a God. Because we are constantly challenged.

And that's okay. God created us that way.

So, when I took the one-dollar socks back, yes, it was a mindfulness moment. But that moment was cultivated over years of practice. Years of saying blessings, years of focusing on giving instead of taking.

NIKKI: How does someone who's never had that, who's never had a religious life, come to this level of mindfulness? To that moment where they say, "It may be one dollar, but it ain't my one dollar?"

THE ATHEIST WHO CALLED A RABBI

RABBI ELI: First of all, it's not hard. There's a God in the world, and everybody knows it, consciously or subconsciously. There's a higher power. As long as you're breathing, you have the obligation—and the opportunity—to investigate that idea. And God has ways of nudging us.

I'll tell you a story from last week.

I got a call from Central Synagogue: There's a Russian Jew in palliative care at St. Vincent's Hospital. Could I go?

It was five in the afternoon. I had the baby in one hand, I was cooking dinner with the other, and the kids were all around making noise, doing homework, being kids. And my wife knows that when it comes to these things—I'm out the door. Not because I'm not dedicated to them, but because this is my calling.

It's also an important lesson for the children: Dedication to someone at the end of life is a priority. If it were someone I could visit tomorrow, I'd go tomorrow. But someone in palliative care, saying goodbye—I need to go now.

I dropped everything—not the baby—and raced to the hospital.

When I got there, there was an elderly man, unconscious, breathing slowly and heavily. Critical. His wife, his daughter-in-law, and her teenage son were there. They told me the patient's son was in another room, resting; he'd been by his father's bedside for hours.

I explained to the family that we would do certain prayers. These prayers cover two bases: If God has decided this is the time, they help with the transition to the next world; if he is meant to live longer, they ease pain and, hopefully, help him return. They were the same prayers I said for you when you were in the ICU.

As I'm praying, I have this stupid voice in my head: "Maybe they don't want me. They didn't call our Chabad Russian synagogue; they called Central. Maybe they wanted a different rabbi." My own insecurity talking.

I turned to the grandson and asked, "By the way, how did you get to Central Synagogue?"

And he blurts out, "I'm an atheist . . . but, but . . . standing here watching my grandfather, I felt that—I don't know—I had this nudge from Hashem, from God, to call a rabbi."

That line jogs something deep and profound in me.

Think about that. Someone who declares, "I'm an atheist," and in the same breath says he had a calling from *Hashem*.

I'm musing in my head, thinking, "That's typical for us humans. We struggle. But the God-connection is already inside and live-wired."

Anyway, he told me he went out to the nurses' station and said, "I need a rabbi." They Googled "rabbi" and Central Synagogue came up first. So they called them.

In that moment, I saw how carefully God orchestrates every connection. We just have to allow God into our lives, and He will perform miracles—from the big ones to the small ones like the story of the one-dollar socks.

NIKKI: It wasn't personal at all . . . even rabbis, good ones, have doubts.

RABBI ELI: Yeah, that's true. . . .

Then, the patient's son comes in—I can see from his face, his pain, he's clearly in need of support. I did what my training taught me: I turned to the boy and asked, "Have you ever put on tefillin?"

"No."

"You never had a bar mitzvah?" I ask the boy.

"No."

I told them a story: A non-Jew once came up to me after a wedding and said, "I finally understand the secret of Jewish survival. At the peak of the wedding, the happiest moment of the young couple's life, what do you do? You break a glass to remember the destruction and the sorrows of the Jewish people. How you combine joy and sorrow in one moment is inexplicable to me—but it explains everything about you."

Then I said to the family grieving their dying father, "We have an opportunity right now. Your grandfather is dying, there isn't much time, but you can have a bar mitzvah here. Now."

And this young man, this "atheist," said, "Rabbi, I'll do it."

He put on tefillin. He said *Shema*, the holiest prayer. I held hands with him, and we danced, right there beside his unconscious grandfather's hospital bed.

I said, "There is no greater joy for your grandfather's soul right now than to be present at his grandson's bar mitzvah."

The father got up and put on tefillin too. We sang together. The next day, his grandfather peacefully passed away.

This was a powerful moment for these three generations of men. A moment. A sacred ceremony. A gift and something being taken away.

They couldn't stop thanking me. But it wasn't me. They were thanking Hashem for putting the right person in the right room at the right time.

NIKKI: I am very moved by this story. As you've often said, "A Jew is a Jew is a Jew." This story illustrates so powerfully that every human being has a spark of God within them. A boy who calls himself an atheist calls on his traditions to sanctify the moment and to give his grandfather an ancient gift—the bar mitzvah, the making of a man. As a secular woman, who sometimes struggles with these "*rules*," I see the beauty and reverence of this tradition.

RABBI ELI: Yes, there's doing all the mitzvot, the daily devotional tasks. I struggle with that like everyone else. I'm not a saint.

But there's another side: being sensitive to what God wants from you in the moment and allowing yourself to be a vessel. Available. That space isn't reserved for "religious professionals." Anyone can be that channel.

KEEPING OURSELVES ACCOUNTABLE

Training your conscience on the "small stuff"

JEWISH ROOT: In our conversation, Eli talked about the one-dollar socks at Kmart—how he almost walked out with them, then caught himself: *"It may be one dollar, but it ain't your one dollar."* In Jewish law, there's no difference in principle between stealing a small amount and a large amount. You don't refrain from stealing because "it harms someone"; you refrain because **God said so.** The line is absolute.

This exercise helps you notice and repair all the "soft stealing" we may have normalised or shrugged off.

For the next **twenty-four hours**, pay radical attention to the grey areas:

- At the supermarket self-checkout
- Using someone else's Netflix/streaming login
- Overreporting your work hours

- Downloading content you didn't pay for
- Taking hotel items that aren't meant to be taken (no, not the shampoos, they're okay, but the bathrobe)

Each time you face a micro-decision, ask:

Is this mine? Or am I just hoping God won't notice?

Jot quick notes in a journal or your phone. No judging yourself—just honest data.

Making a *cheshbon hanefesh* (soul-inventory)

At the end of the day, sit quietly and review:

- DID I CROSS THE LINE—OR COME CLOSE?
- WHAT STORY DID I TELL MYSELF TO JUSTIFY IT?
  - "They're a big company, they won't miss it."
  - "Everyone does this."
  - "I'm too tired to go back, it's just beans."
- HOW DID IT FEEL IN MY BODY?
  - A little jolt of guilt?
  - A dull heaviness?
  - Numbness?

Jewish law loves **teshuvah**—not just regret, but *return* and repair.

Choose **one** thing from your list and do a concrete act of repair:

- Go back and pay for the undercharged item.
- Delete the pirated file and purchase or borrow it legally.
- Email or tell someone: "I underpaid / took X by mistake—how can I fix it?"

Then say (in your own words):

> *I'm choosing to live as if nothing is "too small" for integrity. Even one dollar is not mine if it's not mine.*

Using giving to inoculate yourself against stealing

JEWISH ROOT: Eli explained that Judaism doesn't only say "don't steal"; it teaches you to become the opposite type of person: a **giver, not a taker**. The practice of **tzedakah** (righteous giving) and **ma'aser** (a 10 percent tithe) trains the heart away from grasping and towards justice.

For everybody, this is a beautiful spiritual technology.

MAP YOUR "MONEY FEAR"

Answer these questions in writing:

1. When do I feel most afraid about money?
2. When I imagine giving money away, what's my first feeling? (Fear, resentment, joy, pride, anxiety?)
3. Do I secretly believe: "If I give, I'll have less?" Or do I leave room for the idea: "If I give, my life becomes larger?"

Be very honest. This is your starting point.

CHOOSE YOUR PERCENTAGE

Jewish law speaks about **10–20 percent** for tzedakah, with 10 percent as a standard baseline. You don't have to start there—but choose a clear, concrete practice:

- If you're new to this: start with **1–3 percent** of your monthly income.
- If you're already giving, but irregularly, formalise it into **a fixed percentage**.

The exact number matters less than the **consistency** and intention: *"I am not only a consumer of the world; I am a contributor."*

APPLY THE JEWISH PRIORITY LADDER

Based on traditional tzedakah priorities:

1. **YOUR IMMEDIATE FAMILY** in genuine need
2. **YOUR LOCAL COMMUNITY** (neighbours, local causes)
3. **WIDER WORLD CAUSES** that resonate with your values

Make a simple list:

- One person or family I could help directly: ______
- One local cause I care about: ______
- One wider cause (hunger, education, refugees, mental health, etc.): ______

Distribute your chosen percentage across these three layers in a way that feels balanced and ethical to you.

NO THEFT: A LAW FOR SOULS, NOT JUST FOR SOCIETY

As we closed the conversation, I circled us back to the law itself.

The Noahide command is stark in its simplicity: **Do not steal.**

But what Rabbi Eli drew out with his wisdom and stories is that it is really an invitation into an entirely different way of being in the world.

When Hashem is your operating system, it ceases to become a concrete thought; it's simply the way you are, the way you show up, the who and not the what.

To refrain from stealing is:

- To notice the one-dollar socks, feel the temptation, and say, *"It may be a dollar, but it isn't my dollar."*
- To put down the bag of beans you didn't pay for, even when no one would notice, because *you* would notice—and so would God.
- To refuse to steal someone's time, dignity, or joy through manipulation or gaslighting.
- To tithe, to give, to build communities where people hand each other their supplier lists and say, "We'll buy from you."
- To see laws about tax and rates and secular obligations as **part of God's law**, not separate from it—this way you elevate mundane obligations to God's work on earth.
- To accept that our morals cannot be entirely self-invented. That we are too animal, too desirous, too fragile to be our own ultimate authority.
- To let even an atheist boy hear a whisper at a hospital bed and say, "I need a rabbi."

The Fifth Noahide Law of "no theft" is not a small, miserly command: *Don't touch that, it's not yours.* It is one of the ways God teaches us to recognise that **nothing is really ours**. Not our wallets, not our rings, not even our life-breath.

Everything we "own" is, in Eli's words, "from Hashem"—is on loan, given by God's grace, and is impermanent.

When we remember that, we stop grabbing.

We stop stealing.

We start giving.

And we feel deeply grateful for all that we have and for creation itself. We realise that the world, in God's image, can be a more generous and enlightened place.

CHAPTER 6

What's So Scary About Sex?

NOAHIDE LAW 6: DO NOT COMMIT ACTS OF SEXUAL IMMORALITY

(Love Faithfully)

Set me as a seal upon your heart,
As a seal upon your arm;
For love is strong as death,
Jealousy as cruel as the grave;
Its flames are flames of fire,
A most vehement flame.

SONG OF SONGS 8:6

THE ORIGINS OF THE SIXTH LAW: DO NOT COMMIT ACTS OF SEXUAL IMMORALITY

Of all the Seven Noahide Laws, this one may seem the most personal—and probably the most controversial. The commandment *Do not commit acts of sexual immorality* (and sometimes *"or adultery"* is tacked onto the end) isn't just about prohibiting a list of things we humans like to do in private or in public; it's about protecting the sacredness of intimacy, family, and the human body. In Jewish thought, this law is not about control. It's about covenant.

The roots of this law go all the way back to **Genesis**, before the flood.

In the ancient world described in the early chapters of the Torah, sexual boundaries were fluid and frequently violated. Genesis 6 tells us of a time when *"the earth was corrupt before God, and the earth was filled with violence."* The sages interpret "corrupt" here to mean sexual immorality—where the lines between consent, relationship, and responsibility were blurred or abandoned entirely. The generation of the flood—*Dor HaMabul*—were not just violent; they were morally unmoored.

The prohibition in the Sixth Noahide Law is understood to include: incestuous relationships, adultery, bestiality, rape or sexual violence, and any union that breaks down the sanctity of family or violates covenantal commitment.

But here's what's crucial: This isn't about shame or repression. In Jewish tradition, sexuality is sacred. It's seen as a **Divine gift**, a way for two souls to unite in love, in trust, and in holiness. The first commandment given to humanity in the Torah is *"Be fruitful and multiply."* Sex is not shunned—it is sanctified.

Rabbi Eli said, "Sex isn't dirty in Judaism. It's Divine. But precisely because it's so powerful, it needs clear boundaries."

The Talmud often refers to a concept called *yetzer hara*—the evil inclination—which isn't just about malice or cruelty, but also about unbridled desire, or what Rabbi Eli says is *"the animal soul imprisoning and controlling the higher part of the self."* The tradition doesn't say we should *destroy* this drive—rather, we must elevate it. Use it wisely. Channel it toward life, love, and holiness.

In today's world—where hookup culture, pornography, and the commodification of sex saturate modern media—this law may seem ridiculously out of touch and old-fashioned. But through the lens of our deteriorating birth rates in the West and the disintegration of marriage as the very foundation of society, and crucially, the cheapening of our human connections with each other at the most profound level, perhaps it's more relevant than ever. Because the consequences of sexual immorality aren't just personal—they ripple outward and can tear at the bonds of trust, destroy families, objectify and commodify human beings, and hollow out intimacy.

To follow this law is not to be prudish. It's to be **protective**. Protective of the human soul. Of sacred partnership. Of the idea that our bodies are not playgrounds for impulse, but vessels of Divine light.

A NOTE ON OUR CONVERSATION

When Eli and I recorded this conversation (which turned out to be two weeks before his death), his youngest child was just two weeks old. He was sleep-deprived but ecstatic. It was clear he was completely in love with and devoted to his sweet wife, Chaya, and was alive to the blessings of a large family with five children.

At this point, I was acutely aware of the differences between our life experiences. I fell in love and chose my non-Jewish husband, and while Eli and Chaya chose each other, it was within a strict frame. Neither Eli nor Chaya would have ever considered "marrying out," as I had done.

Judaism, as a matrilineal religion and culture, ensures its survival by decreeing that all children born with a Jewish mother are indeed Jewish. Therefore, my daughter is Jewish, even though my husband is not.

Eli treated everyone the same. He embraced my husband, Rowan, with the same love and affection as he would any brother-of-the-blood, with intense warmth and a ferocious interest in him as a human being and as an aspect of God in human form. That's why everyone loved him.

I met with Chaya at a very tender time, a few days after Eli's funeral, which was packed to the rafters, and she said, "That was a room full of Eli's best friends—literally *everyone* thought he was their best friend." And it's true, Eli had a charisma that could fill a stadium and create fans out of foes and strangers. He made you feel like a giant and that nothing you wanted to do was impossible. It was a great gift.

Out of all our conversations, this was the one where Eli and I disagreed the most. That said, Eli was never judgmental in his tone; he just believed quite simply that the law is the law and, because it was given by God, it's good for you, so you don't disobey it. He wasn't moralising or forbidding, he was presenting a choice. Do you want to live inside the law or outside of it? Do you want to control your animal instincts or let them rip? Do you believe that God's word is the final word and the ultimate good?

For me, it wasn't so black and white. I have gay and nonbinary members of my immediate family, and as a secular Jew, I've had challenges reconciling any prohibitions on expressions of love. To me, that's free will, and I don't want to rein it in (of course, unless it harms others). I believe we live within the embrace of a loving God who brings all things and beings into creation without judgment. Eli and I discussed this, and we allowed each other the space to hold different opinions.

At the end of this conversation, after the recording had stopped, Eli sat back in his chair, sighed, and grinned at me like a kid. I asked him what he was thinking, and he said, "Baruch Hashem, I am blessed. I am completely happy. I love my wife and my children, and I am doing exactly what I am meant to be doing. I am completely on my path."

His childlike glee at his own good fortune made me smile and made me intensely happy and grateful that this joyous man was in my life. Now that he's gone, this memory will be something I treasure in his absence.

ᔕ

NIKKI: If you want to make people uncomfortable at a Friday-night dinner, bring up three topics: money, death . . . and sex. This chapter is about the third one. The Sixth Noahide Law is deceptively simple: **Do not commit acts of sexual immorality.** Think about it—seven little words that run straight into the most complicated parts of being human: desire, loneliness, identity, marriage, children, power, choice. The bits we all struggle with and pretend we don't.

But Eli, stop my mouth from running on! Before we get into the hard stuff, are you getting much sleep with a new baby in the house?

RABBI ELI: Um, yeah, I'd say more than any of the kids. Chaya's doing well. She's really championing this whole deal. The baby's doing well too. So, thank God.

NIKKI: Oh, you have an amazing wife.

RABBI ELI: Yes, I do. Thanks.

NIKKI: And actually, you know, talking about wives . . . let's get back to it. Our conversation today is about sex and relationships and the Jewish approach to that. So . . . how long have you guys been married?

RABBI ELI: It's eighteen and a half years, but in a couple of weeks it'll be nineteen years that we've known each other.

NIKKI: Wow. That is a long marriage.

RABBI ELI: I mean, it feels like yesterday, but yeah, it's a long time.

NIKKI: Was it an arranged marriage?

RABBI ELI: So . . . yes and no. It wasn't like what you see on TV with ultra-Hasidic communities—boy and girl in a living room at eighteen, meet once or twice, everyone says "mazal tov" and done. That exists, but it's not the majority.

For us, it was more guided. There was a matchmaker. There were mutual friends. People who helped us research. But I still chose her and she chose me.

My sister and Chaya were roommates in seminary in Israel. My little sister—not now, she's grown up to be very wise and a trusted friend, but who at the time I would never have trusted with *anything*—comes to me and says, *"Out of all my friends, this is the one."*

And I just . . . blindly trusted her.

NIKKI: Your sister had good taste.

RABBI ELI: Apparently. My sister fell in love with my wife for all the reasons I subsequently did. Her personality is very different, but she'd had a very different upbringing, which made her appealing to both of us.

NIKKI: Tell me more. I don't know much about your background.

RABBI ELI: I'm one of nine children. I have six sisters. The oldest sibling is a boy, and so is the middle, and I'm sort of at the end.

NIKKI: Gosh, your parents were very busy making Jewish babies!

RABBI ELI: I knew that when it came to building my own family, I wanted a stabiliser—someone very solid, very grounded, very loving. And that was Chaya.

NIKKI: Did you fall in love straightaway?

RABBI ELI: No. And that's an important point. We don't "fall in love" the way the movies say. We go in with our heads first. I had a literal checklist—values, character, non-negotiables.

The first time I really understood love was probably a year and a half into our marriage, when I went overseas without Chaya and our first baby. I remember standing in the bathroom, tearing up, and thinking, *"I left my other half at home."*

That's when I realised: *This* is love.

People confuse **lust** and **love** all the time. They go into a relationship heart-first, body-first, and the mind comes in later—if at all. By the time they realise, "Oh, this person's values don't match mine," they're already deeply entangled sexually and emotionally. It's confusing. That confusion is where a lot of heartbreak and a lot of sexual chaos begin.

And that is already part of the Sixth Noahide Law: Don't treat sex like a toy. Treat it with respect, with reverence, like a force of creation. Treat it like God's pact with us.

NIKKI: So, this law is not a list of forbidden acts. It's a framework for honouring the **holiness of human connection.** And in a society that is often confused about what love even means, it brings us back to something ancient, true, and enduring: Real love is sacred. And sacred things must be protected, revered, and held with care. Is that right?

RABBI ELI: Every soul has its match. But when we misuse that gift—when we take what doesn't belong to us, or treat sex like it's nothing—we damage something very deep, in ourselves and others.

THE MIDWIFE WHO WANTED A BABY

RABBI ELI: Just a couple of weeks ago, while Chaya was giving birth, a midwife in her mid-thirties was attending to her. We got talking while they were prepping Chaya, and in five minutes . . . we're talking about her love life.

NIKKI: I can't help laughing here, Eli! Your wife is about to deliver a baby, and you're getting deep with the midwife. That's so you!

RABBI ELI: Yeah . . . I know, so she delivers babies for a living. But all she wants is a family of her own, a child of her own. She's in a ten-month relationship. And he's just told her he's not sure he wants kids. She's devastated.

I asked her, "Do you love him?"

She said, "Yes."

"Is he a good person?"

"Yes."

"Is he kind?"

"Yes."

"Is he ambitious?"

And that's when it all came out—depression, lack of drive—basically, she's his babysitter.

NIKKI: Oh wow. So what did you say?

RABBI ELI: I didn't tell her what to do. I just started explaining our system. How we *start* with values, with the head, and let the heart grow inside a safe structure. And she was amazed. She literally asked me to come and speak to all the midwives.

But before long, she was in tears. She knew, deep down, that her biological clock and her deepest desire—to be a mother—were not aligned with this man. That's not something you can fix with "love is love."

NIKKI: That pain will never really leave her if she gives up motherhood to babysit a man who won't grow up.

RABBI ELI: Exactly. So I blessed her. I said, "I wish you clarity and strength." Meaning: the strength to walk away and find someone whose values align with hers.

APPS, LONELINESS, AND A BROKEN DATING CULTURE

NIKKI: It's not just her. Honestly, I worry about my daughter's generation. Very few of her friends have boyfriends. It seems like the options are either be hyper-independent and not rely on men, or go on apps where half the guys just want sex.

RABBI ELI: I just had this conversation with a family. The dad—who is maybe fifty—tells his son, "Take the dog, walk to a café, meet a girl with her dog, start a conversation." The son and his sister *burst out laughing* at how ridiculous that sounded.

NIKKI: Because that's not how the world works anymore.

RABBI ELI: Exactly. But they weren't laughing because it was a bad idea. They were laughing because they were imagining how other people would laugh at *them* for doing it.

We live in a society where people are so lost that they don't know how to approach one another. Traditional, simple ways of meeting—your dad saying, "Go talk to someone"—have become a joke.

And here is the quiet subtext of the Noahide Law again: When sex becomes detached from covenant, family, and genuine human approach, it doesn't just break rules. It breaks people.

SEX AS THE MOST SACRED ACT

NIKKI: We're told we live in a sexually liberated society—but why does it so often feel like we're more lost than ever? Hookup culture, disappearing intimacy, and a dating scene ruled by apps and algorithms. What was once considered sacred now feels transactional. But what does Judaism actually say about sex? Is it all rules and repression—or is there something deeper, more meaningful, more holy?

RABBI ELI: Sex in Judaism is the **most sacred act**. The most important act of continuity. The first commandment in the Bible is *"Be fruitful and multiply."*

There's such crassness now around the most sacred act. Because it's so sacred, that's why it can fall so low. When something is powerful, it can be used for the highest good or the deepest harm.

The act of a man and woman being together is the only time humans literally partner with God to bring a *new human* into the world. A new creation.

People are meticulous about ingredients when baking a cake. But when they're creating a human being—something infinitely more complex—they're reckless.

NIKKI: Yes. Agreed.

RABBI ELI: Who you sleep with matters. Not just morally, not just physically, but metaphysically. You're shaping a soul's entrance into the world. That's why the Torah sets boundaries:

no adultery, no incest, no bestiality, no exploitation, no casual, disposable sex that treats people as objects. That's what this Noahide Law is about: *protecting the sanctity of life by protecting the sanctity of sex.*

ARRANGED MARRIAGES, DIVORCE, AND DOING THE HOMEWORK

NIKKI: You mentioned once that divorce is actually in the Torah as well.

RABBI ELI: Divorce is a *mitzvah*—a commandment—when necessary. If a relationship has truly broken down and one partner wants out, the other has an obligation to let them go. The low divorce rates in traditional communities aren't because "no one is allowed to leave." They *can* leave. But they often don't need to as much.

NIKKI: Why?

RABBI ELI: For one, we do the homework up front. Before the boy or girl even hears about a suggestion, the parents get a *résumé*—phone numbers of teachers, friends, references. Then they don't just rely on those; they go wider.

They ask: Does this boy have anger issues? Addiction? Does he get up in the morning to pray? Does he have a sense of responsibility? What's the family like? Health issues? Mental health?

It's not interrogation for snobbery or an invasion of privacy. It's care. It's saying: *I know my child. What will give them the best chance of a stable, loving, faithful home?*

My daughter and I have literally sat together and written out traits she wants in a husband: ambition, kindness, stability, and faith. They happen to be exactly what my wife and I want for her too. She trusts us because we raised her with love and strength, not love through weakness.

NIKKI: I confess I'm not comfortable here. It's very foreign to me. I had agency and independence with my choice. I wouldn't have wanted my parents involved at all! And Rowan and I have been happily married for thirty years. Testament enough to my choice of partner and my agency as a modern woman, knowing deeply what's best for me . . .

But I get it from your point of view, you're trying to prevent your daughter from wandering around, wondering if she'll ever meet the right guy.

RABBI ELI: Exactly, that's why she enlisted us. So she doesn't lie awake thinking, "Will I be alone? Do I need a prenup? Will we divorce?"

We don't walk into marriage with a 50 percent divorce statistic hanging over our heads. We walk in with an assumption of **lifelong partnership**, loyalty, children, and a shared mission.

And that stability is part of how the law against sexual immorality protects not just individuals, but whole communities.

"WHAT IF MY CHILD IS GAY?"

NIKKI: So, what happens if one of your kids is gay? Because we all know gay Jews; they're part of our families too.

My nephew is the most beautiful soul. We basically knew at eighteen months that he was gay. I don't want to stereotype him, but by three years of age, the jazz hands and clomping about in his mother's heels were a dead giveaway, and at about eleven, he just said, "I'm gay," and we all went, "Duh."

So what happens in a traditional family when your child is attracted to the same sex?

RABBI ELI: First of all, in the Torah, it doesn't say, "You can't be gay." It says the *act*—sexual acts between men—is forbidden. That's a huge challenge, of course. But it doesn't make a person less than anyone else who struggles with any other sexual temptation—like a married man tempted by another woman.

If my child crossed any line in the Torah, I'd be disappointed, sure, because I want them to have the best path. But I wouldn't stop loving them. You don't project your hurt onto the child. You keep loving them. God gave you a blessing. You embrace them.

NIKKI: We've talked about this book being for "everyone," and everyone includes the LGBTQI community. I don't want to moralise about people's choices.

RABBI ELI: Most gay kids didn't "choose" those feelings. It's how God wired them. I once met, in Israel, a rabbi who runs a group for religious gay men and women. They *want* to stay religious. They want traditional homes, kids, and community. He supports them.

He said to me, "Think of a menorah with seven branches. On one end is absolutely gay. On the other is absolutely straight. Most people are somewhere on the spectrum."

For many people somewhere in the middle, there *is* a way to build a traditional home if that's what they want—especially if they're honest about it when dating, and they put good fences in place.

WHY WE DON'T TRUST "COMMON SENSE" ALONE

RABBI ELI: The Torah is our guide. Who understands humans better than the One who created them? We can't rely on shifting human opinions alone to set the boundaries around sex and intimacy. Let me give you an extreme example.

Hypothetically, there's a woman who never knew her biological father. She meets him later in life. They fall in love. They start a relationship. They decide to have kids through IVF—so the children won't be harmed genetically.

Now, what's your instinctive reaction?

NIKKI: It's wrong. And disturbing. And I'd guess there's a lot of potential psychological trauma there.

RABBI ELI: Of course. We call it incest. The Torah forbids it.

But here's the thing: Fifty years ago, most people in the West also thought homosexual acts were wrong, and people went to jail for it. Now, society has shifted from merely *accepting* to *celebrating* gay people. There are parades. There are slogans like "Love is love" and "It's none of your business what consenting adults do."

So now, if you present this father-daughter case—with IVF to avoid genetic harm—many people say, "Well . . . it's weird, but love is love. Who are we to judge?"

That's how quickly "common sense" can slide.

We can't solely rely on government either. One government says X is wrong, the next says it's right.

The only stable anchors we have are the core values of the Torah—the same values that underpin the Noahide Laws. Not because we always understand them, but because they come from beyond us, from God.

THE NOAHIDE LAW AS RAILS FOR A HARMONIOUS SOCIETY

NIKKI: What I notice about the Noahide Laws is that they're so simple. They feel like common sense rules for society: don't murder, don't steal, don't worship nonsense, don't commit acts of sexual immorality.

If you look at the family court system, it's backed up to the wazoo with broken families, a huge chunk involving adultery or sexual betrayal.

And in older times, incest also made sense to forbid

genetically—because children were often born with terrible disabilities when you "swim in the same gene pool."

RABBI ELI: Correct.

NIKKI: But with this Law, I am genuinely conflicted. I see that the way our society treats sex tears at the fabric of something deep and sacred. But at the same time, I think many of the strides our society has made politically, ethically, and socially for women, people of colour, and minority groups are important, powerful, and humane. I don't want to give those advancements away. If these laws were given to the post-flood world, surely we've evolved since then. I am wondering whether a law like this makes sense in this day and age. To many, it may feel regressive, suppressive, and even cruel.

RABBI ELI: Actually, these human rights that you mention flow directly from the Noahide tradition that we're all created in the image of God. And therefore, we must respect every human being.

But with regard to the Sixth Noahide Law, we don't keep these laws only because they make sense, we keep them because **God said so**. Human common sense is like the wind; it changes with culture.

Let's take, for example, raising kids. A child wants to run into the road or play with a knife. It makes complete sense to them—the knife is cool, the road is exciting. The parent pulls them back, takes away the knife, and the child screams, "You're so unfair! This is my favourite toy."

The parent hears but doesn't listen. They love the child too much to let them destroy themselves.

We are that child. God is that parent. Some of the sexual boundaries the Torah places on all humanity through the Noahide Laws may not feel fair, but they are there to protect our deepest dignity.

MORE THAN JUST SEX: IDENTITY AND SHAME

NIKKI: Do we have this thing in Judaism of being ashamed of sexual behaviour?

RABBI ELI: Interesting question. Shame in Judaism is mainly discussed when *one person shames another.* Public humiliation is compared to murder. God doesn't go around shaming people. You won't find that.

The only time you're meant to feel a touch of shame is privately, in a very organised way—what we call *cheshbon hanefesh*, a soul-accounting. You sit at the end of the day and review: "What did I do? Who am I? Is this me?"

You might feel a moment of shame—not to crush yourself, but to say, "That's *not* who I am. Tomorrow will be different. I will do better." Then you let it go.

I don't think I've *ever* said to my kids, "You should be ashamed of yourself." Ever.

Every morning, we say *Modeh Ani*—"I thank You, living and eternal King, for returning my soul within me." The world is new. I am new. That's actually been my email signature for years: *"The world is new to us every morning, and every person should believe that he or she is reborn each day."*

NIKKI: That's such a different vibe to the shame narrative in popular culture—Eve seducing Adam, the Fall, all of that.

RABBI ELI: Shame as a weapon can be deadly. God doesn't do that. The point isn't to label someone "sexually immoral" and leave them there. The point is: *You are more than your sexual behaviour.*

That includes gay people, straight people, everyone. Society has flattened people down to "I am my sexuality."

Imagine if on your business card, under "Author," it had to say "Heterosexual." Why? Why is sex the headline?

When I meet your nephew, I'm not meeting "a gay person." I'm meeting a person—created in the image of God. That's it. There's so much more to him than who he's attracted to.

CELEBRATING LIFE, MARRIAGE, AND THE UNION WITH GOD

NIKKI: One of the things I love about Judaism is how much we celebrate life—birth, marriage, children. If anyone's ever been to a Jewish wedding, it's like the ultimate party.

How does that connect to this law about sexual boundaries?

RABBI ELI: According to Kabbalah, marriage between a man and a woman mirrors the marriage between God and the Jewish people at Mount Sinai. God is the *giver*, spiritual. The Jewish people are the *receiver*, physical. Two opposites coming together for a higher purpose.

In creation, God—who is utterly spiritual—wanted to interact with something physical. He created a world, a people, a place to be in relationship with.

NIKKI: So, every marriage is like a little replay of Sinai?

RABBI ELI: Exactly. The attraction between a man and a woman is not ordinary. Left to their own devices, men often prefer hanging out with men, women with women. The fact that they're drawn across that divide is something godly. It's beyond logic. That's why it's so powerful and potentially so dangerous.

When a husband and wife come together in love and bring children into the world, they're echoing the original act of creation: two opposites united to bring forth life and light.

And then there's the very mundane side. My wife loves that I've been working from home since the baby. She doesn't need me to breastfeed or change every nappy, but she needs me *there*.

I'm busy thinking about my trips, projects, and trying to fix the "big problems."

She says, "No. You're not going anywhere. There is a baby here. A family. I need you grounded."

That's also part of the holiness of marriage—*being present*, honouring the small things that are actually huge.

NIKKI: It's beautiful. And so Kabbalistic—to link the cosmic and the domestic.

RABBI ELI: That's why we celebrate every life-cycle event. Behind every *brit milah* (the Jewish practice of circumcising baby boys), every bar and bat mitzvah (coming of age for boys and girls at thirteen and twelve years of age, respectively), every joyous milestone in life, what we're really dancing around is that original marriage—the union that brought this child into the world. And behind that, the union between God and humanity.

BRINGING IT BACK TO THE NOAHIDE LAW

By the end of this conversation, I felt like we'd done something subtle but important: We'd taken the phrase *"Do not commit acts of sexual immorality"* out of the realm of slogans and culture wars and put it back where it belongs—inside the story of creation, covenant, and human dignity.

The Sixth Noahide Law doesn't exist to police private pleasure for the sake of cruelty or zealotry. It exists to:

- protect families from betrayal,
- protect children from being conceived in chaos,
- protect vulnerable people from being used,
- protect communities from dissolving into loneliness and distrust,
- protect each of us from becoming nothing more than our hungers.

Judaism insists that intimacy and sex are **sacred**. So sacred that they can't be left to algorithms, "vibes," and whatever your hormones feel like this week. So sacred that, at times, it asks for restraint that feels almost impossible—whether that's a married person walking away from an affair, or someone whose desires don't fit neatly into the traditional structure of marriage.

"Place Me Like a Seal upon Your Heart"—Intention Before Intimacy

JEWISH ROOT: This exercise is about elevating the mundane to the sacred.

Song of Songs gives us a language for holy desire:

Set me as a seal upon your heart,
As a seal upon your arm;
For love is strong as death . . .
Its flames are flames of fire,
A most vehement flame.

—Song of Songs 8:6

In this chapter, Rabbi Eli says that sex is *"the only time where humans are actually in partnership with God to bring another human into the world"*—a new creation. This practice helps a couple bring that consciousness into the bedroom so sex is not casual consumption, but covenant.

1. **SET THE SPACE, NOT JUST THE MOOD**
   - Turn off phones, dim the lights, maybe light a candle.
   - Treat the bedroom like a little sanctuary: not self-conscious, just intentional.

2. **READ A VERSE TOGETHER**

   You can say it in English, or add the Hebrew if you like:

   I am my beloved's, and my beloved is mine.
   —Song of Songs 6:3
   Hebrew: אֲנִי לְדוֹדִי וְדוֹדִי לִי (Ani l'dodi v'dodi li.)

3. **ONE-MINUTE SILENT INTENTION**

Sit facing each other, eyes closed or soft. Each of you, silently:

- "May this be an act of love, giving not taking."
- "May I remember that you are a whole soul, not just a body."
- "May our intimacy bring more kindness and blessing into the world."

4. **EXCHANGE BLESSINGS**

Take turns completing one or more of these:

- "Tonight, I'm grateful for you because . . ."
- "I see God's image in you when you . . ."
- "My prayer for us tonight is . . ."

5. **ONLY THEN, MOVE INTO TOUCH**

Let the physical side flow naturally—but now it's inside a container of intention. This is exactly the opposite of the "casual, mindless, swipe-and-hookup" model.

6. **OPTIONAL: A SHORT CLOSING AFTER INTIMACY**
   When you're lying together afterwards, one of you can whisper: "Thank You, Hashem, for the gift of love and the body."

Or in Hebrew: *Modeh ani lefanecha . . .*—I thank You . . . (echoing the morning prayer that Eli loves: every day, we get to be new).

Sacred "Yes," Sacred "No"—Boundaries as Holiness

JEWISH ROOT: The Noahide Law "Do not commit acts of sexual immorality" isn't just "don't." It's a way of protecting the dignity of love, bodies, and families so society fulfills its Godly potential. Judaism adds a twist: Saying **no** to misuse protects the depth of our **yes**.

> You shall be holy, for I the Lord your God am holy.
>
> —Leviticus 19:2

Holiness in Hebrew (*kedushah*) literally means *set apart*—protected by boundaries.

PART A—CONVERSATION FOR COUPLES
If you're in a relationship, share (only what feels safe) from each column.

- Each partner speaks, the other listens without fixing or defending.

- Agree on **one shared boundary** that honours both of you (e.g., no porn; no flirting/DMs with exes; no sex when either of you is emotionally numb or resentful; regular check-ins).

You can anchor it with the line Eli kept coming back to: *Our morals are not just our own. We're aligning with something higher.*

PART B—PERSONAL REFLECTION (CAN BE DONE SOLO)

Rabbi Eli and I intended to formulate this section, Part B, together. But, time was against us. Elements of it fall outside of the Noahide Laws, but it's inspired by some of the ideas we discussed. It's my take on how to bring more reverence into our intimate lives.

Take a journal and divide a page into two columns: **Sacred "No"** and **Sacred "Yes."**

1. Under **Sacred "No,"** write down:
   - Times you felt used, pressured, or misaligned in love or sex.
   - Situations you *never* want to repeat (e.g., casual encounters that left you empty, staying with someone who toyed with your heart, porn habits that distort real intimacy, affairs, emotional entanglements with unavailable people, etc.).
   - Ask: "Where did I cross my own values? Where did I let someone cross them, and, did I cross God's values?"

2. Under **Sacred "Yes,"** write:
   - Moments when intimacy felt deeply safe, mutual, joyful, and respectful.

- Qualities that make sexual connection feel holy to *you* (e.g., being chosen, safety, exclusivity, kindness, laughter, commitment, emotional presence, spiritual alignment).
- Ask: "What kind of sexual energy do I actually want my life to be built around?"

3. Connect it to the law:

Finish with a short reflection:

- When I read "Do not commit sexual immorality," what it's really protecting in my life is . . .
- The kind of love I want is . . .
- One boundary I am willing to set, starting now, is . . .

"Where God Dwells Between Us"—Emotional and Spiritual Check-In

JEWISH ROOT: The Talmud says:

When husband and wife are worthy, the Shekhinah [Divine Presence] dwells between them.

—Talmud, Sotah 17a

And another passage teaches that there are three partners in the creation of a person: the mother, the father, and God (Niddah 31a).

This is exactly what Rabbi Eli described: intimacy as the sacred partnership between humans and God, and marriage as a mirror of God and Israel at Sinai. This exercise helps couples honour that dimension—even if they're not strictly observant.

STEP 1—CREATE "SACRED TIME" (15–20 MINUTES)

Once a week (many couples like Friday night), set aside a short, phone-free window. You can set the scene with some soft music, pour tea or wine—something that marks this as different from "business as usual."

Read this line aloud (or paraphrase):

When we love and honour each other, the
Divine Presence lives between us.

—Based on Sotah 17a

STEP 2—THE THREE-QUESTION CHECK-IN

Each of you answers, in turn:

1. **HEART**—"Emotionally, this week I felt closest to you when . . ."
2. **BODY**—"Physically, I felt most connected/most disconnected when . . ."
3. **SOUL**—"Spiritually, I sense God/meaning in our relationship when . . ."

Keep it loving and grounded. This is connecting at a level we rarely allow ourselves in our busy lives.

STEP 3—ONE TINY REPAIR, ONE TINY CELEBRATION
Together, agree on:

- **ONE TINY REPAIR** for the coming week

  E.g., "No phones in bed," "We'll hug for thirty seconds before sleep," "If we're too tired for sex, we'll still create a moment of closeness instead of silently scrolling."

- **ONE TINY CELEBRATION**

  E.g., Plan a simple date; choose a night you'll be more intentional about intimacy; write each other a short note of appreciation. You can close with the verse you used earlier:

I am my beloved's, and my beloved is mine.

—Song of Songs 6:3

Or simply:

May our love be a place where God feels at home.

I don't pretend this Sixth Noahide Law is easy. Neither did Eli.

But in his world, and in the Noahide vision, it's not about shame, blame, or judgment, it's about **honour**—honouring your body, your future children, your partner, your own soul, and the God who gave you all of them.

Or, as Eli might have put it: Sex isn't just something you *do*.

It's something you consciously give and consciously receive.

And ideally, it's a gift you cherish—carefully, joyfully—and offer to the One who made you capable of love in the first place.

CHAPTER 7

What Does Justice Look Like?

NOAHIDE LAW 7: ESTABLISH COURTS OF JUSTICE

(Create a Just Society)

You shall appoint judges and officers in all your
gates, which the Lord your God gives you,
according to your tribes, and they shall
judge the people with just judgment.

DEUTERONOMY 16:18

ᔕ

THE ORIGINS OF THE SEVENTH LAW: ESTABLISH COURTS OF JUSTICE

Of all the Seven Noahide Laws, this one stands apart. The others speak to individual restraint—don't kill, don't steal, don't curse God. This one is different. It is communal, outward-facing, and bold. It doesn't simply say *"Be good."* It says *"Build systems that protect goodness."*

The command to establish courts of justice was given to humanity as a whole—not just to kings or judges, but to every level of society. It is, at its heart, a call to collective responsibility.

Before the Flood, the world had descended into lawlessness. The strong preyed on the weak, and chaos reigned. The world that emerged from the seething waters needed something new: accountability, structure, and community. Not just Divine judgment from above, but human responsibility from below. The era of every man for himself was over. In its place, a new vision—a society built on shared norms—one that would provide education, safety, and justice for all.

The prophet Isaiah captures it well: *"God did not create the earth to be a wasteland, but formed it to be a dwelling place."* The sages interpret this as a mandate: Every society must construct a legal and moral framework to uphold the Noahide Laws. Civilization, in other words, is not an accident. It is an aspiration—and one that, like a garden, requires constant tending in order to flourish.

This changes everything. Justice, from this perspective, is not simply a mechanism for self-preservation or social order. It carries a spiritual dimension. Its deepest purpose is to create a society in which **Divine presence** is welcomed inside the tent—it's not just invited to linger at the doorway, but beckoned to cross the threshold and enter fully. And in so doing, create a world large and luminous enough, fair enough, and good enough for God Himself to dwell within.

And God, for His part, endowed human beings with the inherent moral reasoning to work out much of what He left unspoken. We were not left without a compass. We were trusted to build.

That trust comes with obligations. The seventh law calls on us to:

- Appoint judges with integrity.
- Create laws aligned with justice and moral truth.
- Educate our communities on the spiritual, moral, and social value of law.
- Enforce those laws fairly, without corruption or favouritism.
- Ensure due process, the protection of witnesses, and equity before the law.

And proactively build the communal institutions—schools, courts, civic structures—that cultivate a harmonious and thriving society, governed by shared ideals and values, personal accountability, and mutual responsibility.

Why does all of this matter? Because without justice, civilisation collapses. Without courts, the strong dominate the weak. And without a shared commitment to truth, society becomes a playground for cruelty.

"This law is about the soul of humanity," Rabbi Eli says. "A society that stops caring about justice is a society already in decay."

It is the foundation beneath all the other laws—because a moral society cannot rely on individual conscience alone. It must institutionalise goodness. It must put teeth in righteousness. It must insist that wrong be named, that harm be addressed, and that truth be upheld, even when it is costly to do so.

In the Talmud, the concept of *din*—justice—is counted as one of the three pillars upon which the entire world rests. And God is described not only as *Av HaRachamim*, the Father of Mercy, but also as *Dayan HaEmet*, the Judge of Truth. Mercy and justice are not opposites. They are partners.

This seventh law also laid much of the groundwork for the vast tradition of Jewish law—Halacha—a living, breathing system of case law, debate, precedent, and communal guidance that became the forerunner of many of the ethical legal systems still in use today. But Halacha is never merely legalistic. It is rooted in *chesed* (loving kindness), *emet* (truth), and *shalom* (peace). It sees every judge, every lawmaker, every witness as a partner with God in sustaining the moral order of the world.

"In Jewish tradition," Rabbi Eli explains, "a courtroom is a holy place. Not because it's perfect—but because it tries. Its purpose is to hold human actions up to the light." As Rabbi Eli's teacher, the Rebbe, taught—the goal is not merely to make the world a fitting dwelling place for humanity—it is to make it a fitting dwelling place for God.

Today, this ancient law speaks with startling directness to the crises of our age: Corruption in politics, institutions, and the media;

injustice carried out in the name of the law; societies torn apart by tribalism and misinformation; courts that no longer feel sacred and laws that feel weaponised; and a generation of people whose souls are crying out for moral grounding and values worth living by.

This commandment is a reminder that law is not a blunt instrument. It is a sacred trust. Judges are not merely officials. They are stewards of human dignity. And justice—real justice—is nothing less than the architecture for a world fit for God and humanity alike.

Justice in Ancient Israel: When Law Became Sacred

To go forward with this conversation, we must go backward. It's hard to overstate how revolutionary ancient Israel's vision of justice was, not just for its time, but for all time. Rooted in Divine instruction, **law in post-flood Israel wasn't the tool of kings or priests**; it was a **sacred trust**, placed in the hands of every citizen.

What made this possible?

Let's start with the **alphabet**. Unlike Egypt's 3,000 hieroglyphs, the exclusive domain of priestly scribes, or Sumer's 1,500 complex cuneiform signs, the **Hebrew alphabet had just 22 characters.** Phonetic. Simple. Learnable. It made reading the law possible for all—farmer, shepherd, widow, merchant. Ancient Israel may have been the **first truly literate society in world history**, not because it prized education for its own sake, but because it **believed every person had the right to be able to read the law, and, as a result, be accountable to it.**

That principle comes straight from the **Seventh Noahide Law**:

Establish courts of justice. It's the only exclusively proactive commandment among the seven, and it's foundational. Justice isn't just about *not doing harm*, it's about **actively creating a society where right and wrong are known, disputes are resolved, and the vulnerable are protected**. The Noahide Laws, given to all of humanity, culminate in this call: To **build a just society.**

In ancient Israel, that looked like a nation of judges, not kings. The early leaders weren't warriors or aristocrats, but people like Deborah, a prophetess who sat under a palm tree and ruled with wisdom and fairness. Or Samuel, who heard the voice of God but also knew how to listen to the cries of the people.

There were no prisons in the form we understand today. Justice was immediate, visible, and restorative. The goal wasn't to exile people from society forever, but to return them to it—better, repaired, made whole and productive. Punishment came with limits and protections. *An eye for an eye* wasn't really about vengeance; it was about measured compensation. And truth had to be witnessed **by two people**, not whispered behind closed doors, gossiped about in bazaars, or doled out by people on thrones. Justice had rules, justice sought truth, and without overstating it, **justice also had compassion.**

Torah's laws weren't just technicalities; they were moral guardrails. Farmers were commanded to leave the corners of their fields unharvested (*pe'ah*) so the poor could glean with dignity. Every seventh year (*shmita*), debts were canceled, not as charity, but because **no one should be crushed by economic despair.** Every fiftieth year (*yovel*, the Jubilee), land returned to its original families. No dynasty could hoard forever. The system had a built-in reset.

And what held it all together? The court. Not a palace. Not a throne. But a system of people who knew the law, lived the law, and administered it **in the fear of God and love of their neighbour.**

That's what the Seventh Noahide Law calls for—**not courtroom drama, but community-wide integrity**. Every society, says the Torah, *must establish a framework for justice.* Without it, none of the other six laws can flourish.

Why?

To protect life, you need fair courts.

To punish theft, you need proof.

To hold blasphemy accountable, you must define truth.

To prevent cruelty, you must understand boundaries.

And to outlaw idolatry, you must recognise **who within a society, other than God, has the authority to say what is holy and what is not.**

In modern terms, this might sound like civics, ethics, or tort law. But in Torah, it's far deeper.

Justice Is a Spiritual Act

When you build a society where the poor are fed, the powerful are checked, and the innocent are protected, you're not just obeying law, you're imitating God. And you're creating a foundation for society where God has not just a place, but sovereignty.

Because in God's world justice is never cold and remote; it's **fierce,**

warm, exacting, sometimes punitive, but often compassionate. And it flows not from the top down, but from the heart out.

The Seventh Noahide Law is not just an instruction, it's an invitation to build a world where **every life matters**, and every soul can stand tall knowing they can fulfil their worldly and Godly purpose—all under the shelter of law and love.

A Personal Take on Justice and Its Systems

> A NOTE: This fragment is from an earlier conversation I had with Eli before he died. I've included it here because it gives an insight into what he thought and believed about the law.

NIKKI: Hey, Eli you've seen smooth and rough justice up close. What's your take on it?

RABBI ELI: As someone who's seen the inside of the prison system, I've seen people in prison who deserved to be there, and equally, people who did not. Establishing courts means creating a world where the widow, the orphan, the homeless person, and even a stranger has a forum in which they can stand before power and be heard. It also means that punishment, which is sometimes just and sometimes unjust, must be part of the process.

This law isn't just for judges or attorneys. It's for all of us. It asks us every day to reflect:

- Are you honest in your business dealings?
- Do you speak up when someone is wronged?

- Do you believe in truth even when it's inconvenient?
- Are you willing to hold the powerful to account?

Eli said: "Justice may be meted out in the courtroom, but it must **live in the culture**. And when a society makes truth its compass and fairness its creed, it fulfils this ancient, sacred obligation." He believed that:

To establish justice is to imitate God.

To uphold the law is to uphold life.

Notes on Our Conversation

Rabbi Eli and I had our last conversation for this book on the tenth of December 2025. That turned out to be just four days before he was killed. He was running a few minutes late for our chat because, just that morning, he'd been to court in his role as a chaplain for the New South Wales prisons, a role he loved because he believed that that kind of ministering was exactly what he was put on earth to do.

Eli's appearance in court that day had a material effect on the outcome of the prisoner's case. He'd been regularly visiting this prisoner, a man Eli believed should never have been jailed in the first place, because he was struggling with mental illness rather than acting with criminal intent.

The man was freed from jail that day, in part because of Eli's advocacy. The judge was persuaded by two things: Eli's commitment to keep supporting him spiritually after his release, and Eli's willingness to vouch for his character.

Eli was overjoyed that the judge treated the man's sincere pledge to continue his religious learning as a real part of rehabilitation. This was Eli's zone—bringing faith and bringing light.

Eli respected the court with an almost religious reverence. He ardently believed in a system that upheld an ethical code and was proud to be part of it. He said, "The law of the land carries the weight of religious law, but they're often aligned." To Eli there was something deeply sacred in that statement.

❧

Of the two gunmen who opened fire at Bondi Beach, only one survived. One was shot dead by police. His twenty-four-year-old son (whose name I refuse to write) was treated in the hospital for his wounds. At the time of writing, he is being held in Goulburn Correctional Centre, a supermaximum security prison, awaiting trial on fifty-nine charges, including fifteen counts of murder. The Royal Commission on Antisemitism and Social Cohesion will investigate and report on religiously motivated extremism and radicalization and any failings in the policing, security services, and institutions that enabled the gunmen to acquire the firearms used in the attack. And the police and justice system will bring the surviving gunman to court, where he will get a fair trial. To live in a democratic country and believe in its principles is also to believe that justice will be done. If found guilty, the surviving gunman will be subject to the harshest penalties that Australia's laws will allow.

I like to think Eli would have believed in that. And for myself, as the daughter of a judge, I believe in that too.

But what of God's laws? Surely there was a rent in heaven when Eli's soul, which was so violently and prematurely taken from this earthly plane, appeared before God? To answer these questions, in Eli's absence I turned to his most trusted guide and mentor, the venerable Rabbi Yehoram Ulman, Eli's father-in-law and the chief rabbi of Chabad Centre in Bondi, where Eli was his assistant rabbi.

THE SEVENTH LAW AFTER A KILLING

NIKKI: Rabbi, I know that your life has been turned inside out and upside down, but I'm very grateful you've been able to find some time for this conversation. It feels . . . urgent now. We're very close to finishing this book that Eli and I started, and this last Noahide law—establish courts of justice—lands very differently after what happened on December 14. Let's just get straight into it. Could you talk to me about the Seventh Noahide Law and why it's so important from a Jewish point of view—but also why it's so important from a civil society point of view?

RABBI ULMAN: The first six laws, which are universal principles and include the prohibitions against murder, sexual immorality, theft, idolatry, blasphemy, and merciless conduct to animals, are all anchored by the first command—which is to uphold our belief in one God. But God also wanted an upright society to create a *system* to safeguard those laws. And that is what the seventh law is: **Create the communal infrastructure to apply these ideals in**

the real world—which means instituting a legislature, a judicial system, police, and even schools to hold us all to account.

NIKKI: What strikes me as so interesting is that the first six laws are all prohibitions. It's God telling us what *not* to do. And then the seventh law is different. It's an instruction, a positive command, and it feels like a completely different tenor to the previous six.

RABBI ULMAN: Mmmm, that's a very profound insight. Sometimes we think that *not* doing wrong or *not* breaking the law is easy. It's as if nothing's really being demanded of us. We think, "Just don't mess up." But the truth is that it's quite easy to stumble into injustice, social breakdown, and into putting what we want for ourselves ahead of what's right.

So, the seventh law tells us we can't be passive or complacent about turning the world into a Godly place. On all levels, we as individuals and as a society must *feel* that responsibility. And more than that, we must proactively take individual responsibility to act on it. Not just "I will adhere to those six prohibitions," but that we, as a society, will create an *infrastructure* for the world to run according to those principles.

On a small level, where society intersects with us as ordinary humans, Eli was a living example of the seventh law in action—being good, doing good, uplifting the world as an upright citizen should do. He aimed to live by the Rebbe's foundational premise that every single person, and everything that exists, has essential and intrinsic value. He knew that the seven laws are a path to unlocking that value—to rising above the strife and chaos to reveal Divine worth in everyone and everything.

NIKKI: Beautifully said, Rabbi. That's at the personal level, what about the collective?

RABBI ULMAN: Applying this to the macro, the entire world was created so that humanity could work jointly to bring our imperfect world to its perfection—to make it a Godly place and illuminate it with His radiance. Through laboring to implement God's moral code for the world, and through the specific commandments, we're each obligated to do our part to "bring Hashem's presence down to earth."

But in order to achieve that, God imposes something on the whole world: There has to be an ethical, fair, and moral society. Without keeping the Seven Noahide Laws, it's impossible.

Objective Law in a World of Fashionable Morality

NIKKI: So, what does a fair society look like?

RABBI ULMAN: The ideal we aspire to, the perfect world, begins with the recognition that God revealed His code of morality—what is right and wrong—in the Bible. It's objective, not subjective.

A fair society is one in which all its inhabitants are united in achieving this Divine ideal. Not merely to "act" nicely in the way we might each understand it, but according to a unified code. If you make morality dependent on the whims of society—what was right yesterday is wrong today, what's wrong today will be right tomorrow—then everything changes according to the fashions and outlook of each generation. But God's word, that he revealed in the Torah, doesn't change.

NIKKI: It's a very un-postmodern position. I can hear the pushback from Twitter: *Who says your God gets to decide? Whose Torah? Whose morality?* And yet, we clearly don't live in that perfect world.

RABBI ULMAN: No, not yet. In a perfect world, we'd all see the intrinsic value of everything—not just the superficial value. Not the relative value of "what serves me right now," but the inner divinity of each human life, each action. But that's not where we are. So, the Torah takes into consideration that we live in an imperfect world. People do antisocial things. Why? Why do people want to control, to compete, to take away from someone else what belongs to him, to deny someone something that is his?

NIKKI: I think Eli would have said it's because the animal instinct takes over.

RABBI ULMAN: Yes, that's true, on one level. And from that perspective the reason the Torah says we must establish systems is to *protect* society from these tendencies—our baser instincts, as you put it. But really, at our absolute core, every single human being is intrinsically good. We each possess a Godly spark. So, when someone acts immorally, it's not because their true nature is evil or corrupt—it's because a temporary darkness has clouded their vision. They've simply forgotten their own infinite worth.

People often think of a justice system as a cage—a set of restrictions designed to lock up the wild, selfish animal inside of us. But the Rebbe's outlook flips that entirely. These laws—these seven universal guardrails—are actually meant to liberate us, not to contain us.

Judges and Policemen You Shall Place in Your Gates

RABBI ULMAN: In the Torah there is a concept of *shoftim v'shotrim*—"judges and policemen." It understands that even in a perfect society, judges need to exist. When everybody wants to do the right thing, you still need guidance. You need an expert and objective way to assess what's right and what's wrong.

NIKKI: My father was a judge. I understand the necessity of police and judges to maintain a civil society.

RABBI ULMAN: The Torah also speaks about policemen—*shotrim*—because when the negative impulse takes over, and people want to possess at all costs, even if it means stealing or inflicting harm, then you need enforcers—people who make sure others don't overstep the boundaries and trample the rights of others.

When the Seventh Noahide Law says "Establish courts of justice," it means: Create a system that **both teaches *and* protects.**

NIKKI: There are movements across the Western world now that oppose the police and feel justice is not served in the court system.

RABBI ULMAN: Yes. Sadly, there are movements in that direction today—but we look forward to a time when society will reach a level of security and mutual respect that would render many of the disciplinary elements of the justice system unnecessary. It's clear we're not there yet, but a functioning legal system must be a priority for society, even if it's not perfect.

Jewish Law and the Law of the Land

NIKKI: Can you explain how the Jewish court, the *Beit Din*, intersects with the law of the land? In Australia, in the United States, and wherever Jews live under secular law—how do those things fit together?

RABBI ULMAN: In Jewish law, there's something called a *din Torah*—a religious case—when people come to a *Beit Din*, a rabbinical court, to adjudicate a dispute. In modern society, if you sue someone, it's a hostile act. It means, "We're enemies now." In religious communities, people would go to din Torah almost as friends. They'd say, "We don't want to keep any money that isn't ours. There's a grey area in our business dealings. We're going to court to make sure I'm not stealing even one extra dollar that belongs to him."

But overall, when it comes to jurisprudence, civil, and monetary laws, the Beit Din's power is limited to the degree to which the parties might voluntarily place themselves under their authority. If two people come to a Jewish court and sign an arbitration agreement, that agreement is recognised by the secular courts—

not because it's Jewish, but because *any* properly constituted arbitration is recognised.

Today, most of our rabbinical work is either arbitration or highly specialised halachic areas over which a Beit Din still holds significant authority—such as divorce documents, conversion, and complex questions of medical ethics.

NIKKI: So, where do you see the seventh law fitting into our modern world?

RABBI ULMAN: In a perfect society, the legal structure should be a Divine structure based on unchanging biblical principles, and not on what each individual society decides about what's right and wrong. That's the ideal.

But, the Torah recognises that we live in an imperfect world where we haven't reached that level. It tells us through the seventh law that not only is there value in society's laws, but there's actually an obligation on every person to adhere to them. In a deep sense, the entire legislative process, from the individual all the way up to the highest court in the land, can actually be a way of fulfilling this seventh law.

NIKKI: You said earlier that Torah law is eternal, perfect, and from God. Some of those laws, in today's world, could look arcane or outdated. How does the Torah adapt to the modern world?

RABBI ULMAN: We believe passionately that it's not the case that Torah law is archaic. When a human creates a legal system, it's limited to a particular time and place and can become outdated. But with God in the frame, that's impossible.

The Torah can be as modern as any modern society. It doesn't need to adapt—because it contained everything from the very beginning.

In my position, dealing with specialised areas of Jewish law, we deal with some of the most cutting-edge areas of science: fertility, egg donation, surrogacy, and end-of-life issues like organ donation when the brain is dead but the heart can be ventilated. All of this is twenty-first-century medicine. And yet every single question has its precedents and foundations in the Talmud and the codes. Even genetics.

NIKKI: Rabbi, earlier in the book Eli mentioned that the "law of the land is the law." What do you say to that?

RABBI ULMAN: There is a very important Talmudic principle: *dina d'malchuta dina*—"The law of the kingdom is law." It means there is a Torah obligation on a Jewish person to adhere to the law of the land—provided it does not contradict the Torah.

For instance, when a regime issues edicts to criminalise fulfilment of the Torah's commandments, then this rule does not apply. In the Soviet Union, there were attempts to ban circumcision, to ban ritual slaughter, to suffocate Jewish life, to prohibit Jewish education. In cases like that, we created underground schools and facilitated Jewish practice. And similarly, throughout our long history. If we look back to ancient Greece and the story of Chanukah, the Maccabean rebellion began when their enemies made Jewish life impossible—defiling the Temple, defiling Jewish women, prohibiting kosher food and circumcision. If you're going to crush our connection to God . . . that's when we rebel.

Thankfully, this level of oppression is nearly unimaginable for us now in the Western world—and beautifully, it's one of the reasons that, for nearly the first time in our history, we can safely and openly share the Noahide code with the world.

When the System Itself Is Unjust

NIKKI: You and Eli both dealt with people inside the legal and prison system all the time. How do you see our legal system in practice?

RABBI ULMAN: We recognise that secular legal systems are *imperative*—without them, society becomes a jungle. But we've also seen up close that they're not perfect.

NIKKI: Eli was very fulfilled by his work with prisoners, even though he saw a lot of harshness in the system. Does Jewish law prescribe prison sentences?

RABBI ULMAN: The closest thing in the Torah to prison is the law of *arei miklat*, "cities of refuge" for manslaughter. It was not a warehouse of violence. The person who killed unintentionally had to go live in a Levitical city—among the most moral, ethical people in society. It was exile, it was accountability, but it was also rehabilitation.

The Torah has a lot to say about *teshuvah*, the path by which we can return to God, and it's generally considered to be part of the Noahide code. You can see it like this: God wants us to regret our actions, resolve to change, and reenter society in a positive way.

But to answer your question, Judaism does not use prison as a default punishment. Prison is only justified to protect society from someone dangerous. The punishment has to fit the crime. For white-collar embezzlement or other financial crimes, the punishment is monetary and restorative. The idea is to make the victim, and the perpetrator, whole.

Protest, Free Speech, and When Words Become Weapons

NIKKI: How do we, as a modern secular society, deal with activism, protest, free speech, from a Noahide perspective? Especially with the level of antisemitism we've seen since October 7. The world is intersecting with the Jewish world in a way it hasn't since the Holocaust.

RABBI ULMAN: Generally speaking, we have to be very careful not to stifle freedom of speech. At the same time, when freedom of speech poses a danger, when it exceeds boundaries and threatens society, we must limit it. Speech leads to action. We've seen that it can begin with words and finish with violence.

So just as we stop physical violence, we must stop incitement—speech that calls for violence or dehumanises others. That's part of the responsibility of society under the Seventh Commandment: to create a legal system that protects the other six Noahide Laws.

NIKKI: Eli also talked earlier in the book about another category of speech that is morally forbidden but very hard to prosecute—lashon hara—evil speech, gossip, destroying reputations. He said it can destroy lives in ways you cannot repair.

RABBI ULMAN: I'll tell you a story: A man came to a rabbi and said, "Rabbi, I want to do teshuvah—repentance. I've spoken badly about people. How can I fix it?" The rabbi told him, "Bring a feather pillow." The man brings it. The rabbi cuts it open and throws the feathers out the window. The wind carries them everywhere. Then the rabbi says, "Now go collect every feather." The man says, "Rabbi, that's impossible." And the rabbi says, "Exactly. That's lashon hara. Once you release it, you cannot take it back."

NIKKI: So even if we can't always enforce laws against such speech, we have to teach society about the damage it does. This Noahide Law about justice is not only about courts; it's about education and it's about building a culture in which people know that words have power.

Protest as a Mitzvah

RABBI ULMAN: As for protests, in a perfect society, there's no dichotomy between legal speech and moral speech. They're the same. Even if something isn't prohibited by law, people intuitively know it's wrong. But we're not there yet. So inevitably, you'll have protests that are justified and protests that are not. Judaism definitely makes room for nonviolent protest.

NIKKI: On what basis?

RABBI ULMAN: On the commandment to *rebuke*—to speak up when something is wrong. The Seventh Noahide Law is the collective form of that: Don't say, "As long as I live the right life, I don't care what happens around me." We're obligated to care about what happens around us. If something is not right, we should roll up our sleeves and **get involved**. In a way, to protest is to express the essence of the seventh law—it's a way for the people's voice to say: "This law is not being kept. This is not justice."

Of course, not every protest is good simply because it's loud. We're talking here from the premise that God gave us an understanding of what's right and wrong, and we're amplifying the right, the just, and the good. Once a person has that, it's their duty to influence the world around them—family, friends, community, or, if they have the power, legislation itself.

NIKKI: I like that—that this Noahide law includes telling truth to power.

RABBI ULMAN: There is a story in the Torah: The daughter of Jacob, Dinah, was raped by the prince of Shechem. Two of her brothers punished not only the prince but the whole city. Why? One of the interpretations is that under the Noahide Laws, the entire society is obligated to create, participate, and uphold justice. They allowed such things to happen, they looked away. The whole Seventh commandment is based on this idea: Every single person must step in where justice is absent, even if there are no formal courts.

Justice in Heaven and Mercy on Earth

NIKKI: What about justice in heaven? Is there a reflection, in God's realm, of what we do on earth? Is it micromanaged—how do you see it?

RABBI ULMAN: It's a very difficult philosophical question. The Talmud tells us that when God created this world, it could not function if it was run solely according to strict justice—*midat ha-din*. If every wrong act was punished immediately and precisely, the world would not survive.

Because God is hidden in this world, He doesn't reveal Himself in an obvious way; He leaves room for faith, for free will. He said, "I cannot run this world by strict justice alone. I must combine it with mercy—*midat ha-rachamim*."

Human courts must aim for justice. Sometimes they can facilitate compromise in civil cases, which is a kind of mercy. But they cannot say, "We feel sorry for this murderer, so we won't punish him." That would break society.

NIKKI: What about in God's realm?

RABBI ULMAN: In the world to come, Divine justice is perfect. Everything is measured according to truth. But because God knows everything—every test, every trauma, every unseen factor—His perfect justice contains perfect mercy. He can distinguish between two people who committed the same act but not from the same place. We cannot. So yes, there is justice in heaven. But on earth, we must do the best we can with partial information.

Eli's Death, Revenge, and Punishment

NIKKI: Some questions are not theoretical. So, given that . . . and obviously this is a very challenging question for you, because of the grief and the closeness of it . . . How do you reconcile Eli's death with perfect justice in God's universe?

RABBI ULMAN: I'm just thinking how to articulate it . . .

First, we need to distinguish between revenge and punishment. Revenge is the wrong word for what justice is meant to be. Revenge is about satisfying one's urge to "get even."

After October 7, or after December 14 here, a person might say, "If I could get my hands on a terrorist, I would cut him limb by limb." Why? Not because he's motivated by a Godly, altruistic idea of cleansing evil from the world, but because he wants to satisfy his own animalistic desire to make the terrorist suffer at least as much as he made others suffer. That is revenge.

NIKKI: And what about punishment? My lower self, the part of me that is hurting and trying to make sense of Eli's death, maybe there is a part of me that wants justice, not just human justice, but Divine justice.

RABBI ULMAN: Punishment is different. Punishment, as the Torah sees it, says: This world is not a jungle, we are not animals.

Certain actions make a person undeserving to continue to live in this world. Not because we are bloodthirsty, but because murder, for example, is the most destructive crime to society.

NIKKI: What about atonement? That's a Jewish concept, right?

RABBI ULMAN: Atonement is a very tricky subject. Some people do not deserve atonement; some do. I want to be very careful here; it's much deeper than I can say in a few sentences. But in principle, yes, in some extreme cases, capital punishment is the Godly form of justice. A human is created in the image of God. So, to murder another human being is to desecrate God. It's really the ultimate destruction of the social and moral contract that binds us all. The murderer should forfeit their God-given role in society.

NIKKI: In Australia, we don't have capital punishment. Do you feel that justice will be done to the man who killed all those people—the surviving gunman?

RABBI ULMAN: I believe it will *not* be done, because he will continue to live. And because he continues to live, there is the possibility of his coming out one day or at least living a life behind bars, and that is still . . . life.

But we live in the system we live in. So, I hope, at the very least, that in this case they will give the Bondi gunman life without parole—that he will never be able to use any legal avenue to come out.

Who Gets to Forgive?

NIKKI: We talk about forgiveness, a word that gets thrown around casually in op-eds whenever Jews are asked to swallow the unthinkable. Something you mentioned before about mercy and forgiveness—how does Jewish law hold those things together? There's the law, and then there's mercy and forgiveness. How do you connect them?

RABBI ULMAN: If forgiveness is offered by a third party, it is neither justice nor mercy. It is theft.

NIKKI: Theft?

RABBI ULMAN: Yes. Only the person who was harmed has the right to forgive. So, when someone says, "We forgive the Nazis for killing six million Jews," that is meaningless. We can't forgive on behalf of the dead. We can't forgive on behalf of another victim. That right belongs to them alone.

When Morality Falls Apart

NIKKI: So, in this world where our morality is so fractured and many people can't even see that hate speech against Jews is unacceptable—how do we, as a society, come to judge these things? How do we make clear—and this is obviously one of the aims of this book—what is right and wrong? Because we're living in a crazy world where people have an argument for everything.

RABBI ULMAN: I hear your question loud and clear. Again, the only way to get it right is if you accept that morality is not subjective. It is objective. That's the only way. To know that only the Bible can give you the answers to those questions. If you don't use the Bible, you can get it right, you can get it wrong—but it will never be perfect.

We live in a world where most people don't yet accept that all morality comes from **that Source.** So, we have to count our blessings and hope that, in most cases, they'll still get it right. We are fortunate that in a large portion of the Western world, they do understand this imperative—at least in many instances.

Light Among the Nations in a Dark Time

NIKKI: I've often heard it said that the Jewish people were chosen for this mission—**to be a light among the nations**. How do you see our role now, in the modern world? I mean, since October 7. Before that, we were all very quiet. We were living our lives. As a secular Jew, I wasn't particularly thinking about being Jewish. But now it's all I think about. I feel like the Jewish world has collided with the Western world in a way it hasn't since the Holocaust. What do you think is our mission going forward? Because clearly . . . it has shifted.

RABBI ULMAN: Our mission as Jewish people is, first and foremost, to rededicate ourselves and commit ourselves as much as possible to the principles of Torah and Judaism.

When I say "as much as possible," I don't mean the Torah is negotiable. We can never tell a person, "Don't worry, just pick the laws you like and ignore the rest. We have to be honest. The Torah is not negotiable. Everything is given to us by God, and everything ultimately must be kept.

At the same time, we recognise that there is an intrinsic value in every single mitzvah on its own. That's the beauty of what the Lubavitcher Rebbe taught, and what all of us as his disciples and ambassadors try to live—and that's what Eli did every day of his life—amplify good.

NIKKI: I think of Eli bringing light into a dark hospital corridor, or coaxing a half-lost boy to put a coin in a charity box.

RABBI ULMAN: When the Jewish people dedicate themselves to the principles of Torah—which includes not just the rituals, not just our responsibilities and obligations to God, but equally our obligations to our fellow human beings—such a person creates a *kiddush Hashem*. He sanctifies God's name by his very presence, by what he does. That was Eli.

That's what I wrote on Eli's tombstone.

Tombstones are very . . . delicate in Jewish law. You can't just write emotional things. You can't exaggerate. Everything has to be factual, chosen very carefully to encapsulate the person's service to God. I wrote that he sanctified God in his life and in his death. Because that's who he was. He brought God's name into hospitals, into prisons, into shopping centres—just as the Rebbe's mission encouraged him to do.

When a person lives a life of integrity and kindness as a religious Jew, as Eli did, people say, "If that's what it means, maybe

I want to come a little closer." Maybe they won't become exactly like him, but they'll do another mitzvah, be a bit more open.

That's our job. Our job as Jews is to sanctify God's name through the way we connect to God and through our conduct toward people. By doing that, we bring light to the nations. Because then people are willing to hear what we have to say

Where the Seven Laws Fit in the Jewish Map

NIKKI: So, in the hierarchy of things—because obviously there are 613 laws a Jew needs to pay attention to—where do the Ten Commandments and the Seven Noahide Laws fit into that? How do we determine the hierarchy?

RABBI ULMAN: The Seven Noahide Laws are for everybody. They're like large houses that have rooms for other additional laws and commandments. The same applies to the Ten Commandments. They're central laws because each commandment is not just a single commandment—they're a kind of *general category* that contains many other things. For example, Shabbat is connected to belief in creation, belief in God's involvement in the world—central tenets of Judaism.

And there's a significant overlap between the Seven Noahide Laws and the Ten Commandments—though not universal because there are laws in each that don't exactly overlap. Charity, for example, is not listed as a separate Noahide commandment, but the Talmud treats it as a given that a decent person must give charity. You must share what God has given you. So, we encourage everyone to give charity. It makes them better people and encourages them to keep the other laws. It strengthens their moral sense. It's a bridge into the seventh law—helping to build a just and compassionate society.

My Second Chance

NIKKI: I really want you to know that I feel incredibly lucky to have had two miracles. One was that I got a second chance at life. And the second was that Eli came into my life and ignited my Jewish soul.

I feel absolutely that this is my mission now—to bring his light into the world, as he did for me. I truly believe I wouldn't be here if he hadn't interceded on my behalf to God. I got a second chance, and I will not squander it. I want to do his work in the world, through my writing, through this book.

RABBI ULMAN: Since you became part of Eli's life, you're part of our life. Because we are Eli's.

NIKKI: Sorry, Rabbi Ulman, I didn't mean to get so . . . emotional.

RABBI ULMAN: I hope you continue the connection.

NIKKI: Oh, I have every intention. He was gently enfolding me into the community over time. With or without this book, he wanted to bring my family and **me into his world**. That has happened.

And now, together—as two families united in the same mission—we can make sure his legacy lives on. I feel this so strongly for his children. That they'll have something in written form, which is so intrinsic to Judaism, to be educated, to have words that celebrate his life. I really hope this book will be something precious for them as they grow up. That they'll have their father's words.

REREADING THE SEVENTH LAW AFTER DECEMBER 14

As we wrapped up, Rabbi Ulman looped back to where we began—not in the courts of heaven, but in the streets and prisons and parliaments of earth. A society that obeys the Seventh Noahide Law is not one with perfect angels and flawless judges. It is one where:

- Law exists, not lawlessness—society is not a jungle.
- Justice aspires upward—toward an objective code, not just popular taste.
- Institutions build communal support—we can't rely on individual moral instincts.
- Individuals are responsible, not just institutions—they protest, rebuke, advocate, and refuse to look away.
- Courts protect the weak, not just the rich who can afford the best lawyers.
- Punishment is about protecting life, not indulging revenge.

- Education proactively transforms society—we must reach forward into the future with educational systems that support justice and fairness for all.
- Words are treated as powerful, not weightless—because feathers scattered on the wind do not come back.

I left the conversation that day carrying two things at once: grief that we had to have this conversation because Eli was gone; and a strange kind of steadiness, knowing that the law he loved, the law he upheld when he visited prisons and hospitals and courtrooms, did not die with him. Eli said, "*Establish courts of justice* is not only about judges, benches, and legal codes. It is about each of us deciding whether we will be part of the jungle, or part of the garden."

And in a world that is again asking what it means to be just, to be safe, to be human, the seventh law is not archaic at all. It is the question on which everything else now seems to turn.

A NEW CONNECTION HAS BEEN MADE

At the very end of a long conversation, I saw Rabbi Ulman smile, a smile of relief and perhaps wonder, as he reflected on the son, friend, and colleague he had lost. For a moment, the conversation slipped into logistics—deadlines, introductions, corrections, eulogies to be transcribed and possibly turned into an afterword. There are emails and publishers and printers waiting for dates.

But under all that, the real text of what we're doing in this chapter is simple:

Two Jews, one religious and one "less observant" (as Rabbi Ulman suggested to me), trying to sketch, in human words, what a just society looks like when the world has shown us its worst.

Trying to honour the Seventh Noahide Law is a noble pursuit—especially at a time when we have seen, up close and personal, what happens when morality fails, when words are weaponised, when justice is delayed or distorted, and when two men with guns step onto the glazed sands of Bondi Beach and tear a hole in the world.

It started with Eli and me, and in an unbroken chain, now connected with Rabbi Ulman, we are writing, together, for Eli's children and for yours, for Jews and non-Jews and anyone else who suspects that "Don't kill, don't steal, don't torture animals, don't worship idols, don't desecrate the Name, don't betray love, and build courts of justice" might be the bare minimum we need to keep this fragile thing called civilization from falling apart.

Epilogue

Rabbi Eli Schlanger is dead.

Killed in what *The Sydney Morning Herald*, one of Australia's most widely read newspapers, called "the worst terrorist attack ever on Australian soil." Ten-year-old Matilda (surname withheld) died in that attack too. As did eighty-seven-year-old Holocaust survivor Alexander Kleytman. Imagine surviving the Holocaust only to die in a massacre on glorious Bondi Beach in, arguably, one of the safest countries in the world. The tragedy is staggering. The irony is obscene.

Australia, and indeed the whole Jewish world, is in mourning. On New Year's Eve in Sydney, a blue menorah was projected onto the Sydney Harbour Bridge, and a minute's silence was observed in solidarity with the victims and the Jewish community. Gathered along the vast shoreline surrounding Sydney Harbour, thousands of mobile phones rose to form a halo of light, marking the moment with a bleak and sombre reverence.

A cloud of fear has lingered over the city as the story of slain Jews has been front-page news for five weeks. It wasn't helped by the fact that our prime minister, Anthony Albanese, had, since the attack, refused to hold a Federal Royal Commission (a formal, independent inquiry into matters of public importance, such as systemic failures—like this—and to uncover facts and assign accountability). On January 8, under clear duress, PM Albanese relented and agreed to a Royal Commission into Antisemitism and Social Cohesion, but not before the Jewish community, as well as many prominent judges, sports stars, and business elites, signed an open letter published in all the major newspapers pleading for one. Now, as a society, we hope we can come to grips with the tragedy, mourn, heal, make amends, and ensure it never happens again.

Australia is not an antisemitic society, but since October 7, 2023, governments, institutions, universities, arts organisations, and the society at large have allowed an undercurrent of hate to percolate—doxxing, gaslighting, threatening, and intimidating the Australian Jewish community.

Rabbi Eli and I did not set out to write a political book, although we both agreed that being Jewish has always been, and still is, political. We've been human footballs, kicked around by powerful nation-states since we were expelled from Egypt. The pogroms in the Middle Ages decimated Jewish communities throughout Europe, including in the German lands, France, England, and Spain. Between the late 1800s and the early 1900s, hundreds of pogroms swept through Russia. And in the Holocaust, the greatest shame and tragedy of the twentieth century, the most devastating genocide the world has ever known, at least six million Jews were killed.

Today, there are approximately 15–16 million Jews worldwide. There are only 120,000 Jews in Australia.

The figure is important to consider because we're the only

community with bars on our windows and private security at the doors of our hospitals, schools, community centres, synagogues, and nursing homes—and we're still not safe! Premier Chris Minns recently contemplated enlisting the military to protect us. For heaven's sake, this is not okay! The massacre at Bondi Beach was not okay!

But to counter the darkness, perhaps the most consoling and astonishing part of all this destruction and death is the support of the Australian community. A day or so after the massacre, a plane flew over Bondi trailing a banner with the words: "From Aus for our Jewish community." On Sunday, January 4, at the Ashes Test between England and Australia at the Sydney Cricket Ground, to a crowd of more than forty-eight thousand cricket fans, the names of the fifteen victims accompanied the words "Forever in Our Hearts" emblazoned on screens. The entire stadium jumped up to a rapturous standing ovation as a group of first responders led a procession onto the pitch to celebrate Ahmed al-Ahmed, the Syrian-born man who helped disarm one of the gunmen, and Chaya Dadon, a fourteen-year-old Jewish girl who was shot in the leg while trying to shield two children she didn't know from the bullets.

Today, January 22, the circle has closed, not just for me, but for the victims' families, the Jewish community, and the nation as a whole. To mark the formal end of the Jewish mourning period (the Sheloshim—officially on the thirtieth day), Australia held a National Day of Mourning. To commemorate the day, Australian and Aboriginal flags were flown at half-mast; prayer vigils were held in churches, synagogues, and community centres; and Australians were encouraged to light candles and set them in their windows as a symbol of fellowship and respect. At 7:01 p.m. the nation observed a minute of silence. It was a fitting and solemn reminder of the day darkness broke forth from the underbelly of human intolerance and hate, and Australia lost its innocence.

Rowan and I attended the memorial for the victims and their families held at the Sydney Opera House. The politicians promised "Never again," and although we've all heard those words many times, too many times, the crowd roared with optimism and hope for the future. This is the Jewish spirit. This is who we are.

As I sat in the Opera House, one amongst a huge crowd, I felt a sense of relief and release. I felt that for the first time since October 7, that I, and many Australian Jews, were waking up to the fact that we are not alone—that the vast proportion of the Australian community does not hate us. They may not understand us, they may never have met one of us, but they don't hate us, and they certainly don't wish us dead.

This is their gift to us—those fifteen souls gave their lives to usher in a new age of tolerance and love. Rowan whispered to me during the ceremony, "Australians are good people. In the long run, they won't put up with antisemitism." I hope he's right.

ᔕ

On Monday, December 15, the morning after the shooting, I had a call from a journalist at *The Sydney Morning Herald*, who asked for a quote about who Eli Schlanger, the man and the rabbi, really was. The headline, a direct quote from me, read: "'He Wouldn't Have Hated the Gunmen': Victim Eli Schlanger's Mission Was Love and Light." What was supposed to be a line, a simple quote for a bigger piece on all the victims, turned into a full article on my relationship with Rabbi Eli Schlanger.

Eli and ten-year-old Matilda became the faces of the event. I saw his face flash up on CNN and the BBC, and it was all over social media.

So here we are. Here I am, still processing my grief and trying to come to grips with the horrific events of the fourteenth of December.

The words in this book will never fully convey Eli's energy, his compassion, his humour, or his love for humankind. He was optimism and love personified. One is tempted to deify the dead, but I'm not the only person who felt Eli was a special human.

In his eulogy, Rabbi Ulman said, "Everybody loved him. It was his personality and what he represented."

Alex Ryvchin, co-executive of the Executive Council of Australian Jewry and a friend of Eli's, said in an interview on Chabad.org: "He had something highly unusual and uncommon, just a natural radiance as a human being. He drew people towards him. He did it through something inherent in him, something the Almighty endowed him with. But he also did it with a smiling, cheerful face that you couldn't help but love, a policy of no judgment. It didn't matter to him if you were a Hasidic Jew and observed all the commandments, or whether you were a pork-eating Russian Jew. He treated you the same. His loss is monumental."

Eli and I were friends. Great friends. But we were so much more than that. Eli's role in my survival and recovery from life-threatening pneumonia is so profound that it defies a scientific and quantifiable explanation. The intervention Eli made on my behalf to God, with the prayers he uttered at my bedside in the ICU and the shofar he blew, occurred at the spiritual level of existence, where things cannot be explained or named but can only be *felt*.

As the beneficiary of that intervention, which resulted in a second chance at life, I owe Eli my deepest thanks and most profound gratitude.

But that's not the end of the story.

Another miracle occurred.

Eli and I were three-quarters of the way through *this* book. A book he wanted to "go global—not just for Jews but everyone who wants to live in a just world." Through our conversations, where I learned about the Noahide Laws and investigated my own faith and Jewish identity more deeply, he challenged and changed me and, perhaps unknowingly, perhaps knowingly, prepared me to bring his light to the world through this container—a book with his actual words written down and preserved for eternity.

Eli saved me. Now I'm saving his legacy.

The synchronicity of this is so potent, so extraordinary, and so existentially otherworldly and ineffable, I can only assume God designed it this way. It doesn't make sense in any rational universe . . . except that in the realm of the Divine—where things may be preordained, or at the very least are so mysterious that we have no frame of reference with which to comprehend them—magic and miracles *can* and *do* happen.

Eli handed me his torch. He was lit with an unshakable conviction in God's Divine plan for everything, so much so that he often said to me, "Who are we to dispute God's will and God's plan?"

A magnificent chain has been forged between Eli's soul and my soul, and the soul of every person who reads this book. When you read Eli's words, you are taking in the words of a man who was steeped in God's grace. A man who had absolute faith in God's love for us and a belief that through the Noahide Laws we can do better, try harder, love more completely, and live together in a more harmonious world.

At the beginning of this project, and as a secular Jew, I didn't have Eli's complete and total faith in a benevolent God . . . but I'm getting there. I believe Eli would view this conversion to my own faith as another one of God's miracles. But this miracle I attribute completely to him—his faith was so infectious it was hard to resist. And where it landed, somewhere deep down at the soul level, which bypassed the conscious mind and any objections it may raise, was a place of transformation and transmutation. I am not the same person I was before I met Rabbi Eli.

I believe wholeheartedly that Eli, and his pact with God, brought me back from the brink of death expressly to write this book and fulfil his mission. Sound kooky? It does when I say it out loud. Nevertheless, it's what I feel, and I'm going with the feelings.

Why are we here?

What are we supposed to do with our lives?

How are we to create a more just and safer world for every human being?

These questions are not entirely answered by the Noahide Laws, but they go a long way to doing so.

Eli believed we're currently living in a time of darkness before the age of the Messiah. Might his death be a small part in this great plan?

Only time will tell.

But in the meantime, his death and the deaths of the other fourteen people have already brought great change to Australia . . . and the world.

In a speech to parliament attempting to galvanise support for new hate speech laws, Anthony Albanese said: "Terrorists, inspired by ISIS, murdered our citizens, on our soil. We must face that unforgiving truth and we must learn from it. That responsibility starts with me, as Australia's thirty-first prime minister."

He went on to say: "The defining and enduring truth of that fateful Sunday is not fear or bloodshed. It is not the cowardly antisemitic evil of the terrorists. Nor the murderous perversion of Islam they took as inspiration. It is the courage and kindness of people risking their own lives to save others."

Is this all about Eli bringing light? We can certainly argue that his death wasn't in vain, but it is now up to our leaders to make living in Australia much safer for the thousands of us who are left behind.

For me, I will never stop missing him. I'm twenty years older than Eli, and I had planned that he'd be at my bedside reciting the *Shema* as my soul departed this world for the next.

God had other plans.

Because my relationship with Rabbi Eli Schlanger began on another plane of existence, it is framed there in my mind and my soul. In a daily sense, I am still having conversations with him. Still asking him to answer the big questions. I can't hear his voice in a visceral, corporeal way, but I hear it in my head—words he'd said to me in the past? Maybe? Perhaps me connecting with his soul? I don't know.

This book is a dedication to Rabbi Eli's light and wisdom. It's our combined offering to God and to humankind. Forgive me if these words seem hubristic; I don't mean them to sound grandiose, but that was our intention and shared mission when we began this project. We wanted to create something timeless, meaningful, and useful.

Now it's over to you, the reader, to determine whether we accomplished this rather lofty aim . . .

What would Eli have said?

Simply, Baruch Hashem.

Nikki Goldstein

January 22, 2026

Afterword by Rabbi Ulman

It is very difficult to write about Eli in the past tense.

Painful as it is, though, this is the reality we now face.

Jewish law is compassionate, but it is also disciplined and precise. Even in grief, it prescribes in great detail the proper conduct of a Jewish funeral, burial, the mourning periods, and more.

One of the laws about a funeral pertains to the synagogue.

A synagogue is not simply a gathering place. In Jewish understanding it is a *mikdash me'at*—a miniature sanctuary, a place where we welcome God's presence and engage in intimate prayer to Him. For this reason, Jewish law generally prohibits bringing a coffin into a sanctuary and rarely permits holding a funeral inside it.

There are, however, exceptions.

One of these exceptions is for a person who is regarded as a *kadosh*, a holy martyr.

Eli died a holy martyr, and that's why his funeral service took place in the sanctuary of our newly consecrated centre, into which he had invested his heart and soul.

WHAT IT MEANS TO BE A MARTYR

The word "martyr" has been cheapened in modern language. It is often used to describe a melodrama, a personality type, or as a political slogan. But Judaism is far more exacting.

The designation of "martyr" in Jewish law is reserved for someone whose death becomes a sanctification of God's name—not because he pursued death, God forbid, but because in the final moment, the person is bound so completely to God that even in death he cannot be separated from his mission.

We cannot fathom it. We tremble before it. But the tradition teaches us all a principle: That there is a form of faithfulness so complete that it is not measured by intellect or achievement, but by total alignment with God's will.

And that alignment is what Eli strived to achieve and how he lived his entire life, from moment to moment, dedicated to sanctifying God's name.

My dear son-in-law, Rabbi Eli (whose full name is: Feivel Eliezer HaLevi, son of Rabbi Binyomin HaLevi and Dobra Beila Schlanger—may they live long lives and enjoy endless *nachas* from their children, grandchildren, and great-grandchildren) was not someone you'd describe as saintly or otherworldly. He was very much a man of the people. Words like "piety" and "lofty" are not descriptions that come to mind about him.

Eli was gregarious and down-to-earth, with a perpetual smile and twinkle in his eye. He loved life, was curious about the world, and loved spending time with his family and his many friends.

He had a unique and contagious sense of humour, and people were drawn to him. He simply *loved* people.

Along with all this, Eli possessed a highly refined sense of what true holiness and goodness look like and an inner drive to touch that holiness and to open himself up to that greatness. Eli sought to tap into timeless wisdom and holy energy—and, in that way, become a greater version of himself. He sought to align his mind, his heart, his body, his soul, his inner drives, and all his talents and interests with God, to live his life in sync with what God expected of him.

But how to achieve this? The Torah charges us to "cleave to our Sages" and to learn from them how to serve God and sanctify His name.

With every fibre of his being, Eli "cleaved" to the Rebbe, Rabbi Menachem M. Schneerson, of saintly memory, in whom he recognised a Moses-like figure of daring leadership, selfless love, groundbreaking scholarship, penetrating wisdom, and vibrant inspiration, all contained inside a highly unassuming humility—a man who lived 24-7 in complete alignment with God's will.

He considered it his life's greatest privilege to become an emissary of the Rebbe and to carry the Rebbe's message. He internalised the Rebbe's most oft-repeated charge: "Action—deed—is the main thing!"

Eli's *schlichut*, mission, was to honour the Rebbe's call to care for every individual—with particular emphasis on the forgotten and the downtrodden—and to be sure to communicate to them the unique role they play in God's plan for the entire world.

He strove to fully integrate the Rebbe's teachings about Divine Providence—to recognise in life's every moment and circumstance an opportunity uniquely created and curated by God for that person to utilise and transform. And how much more meaningful and impactful life is when we indeed open ourselves up to the vast presence of that opportunity!

The Rebbe's deep scholarly and mystical treatises about the Divine desire for fusion of the physical and temporal with the holy; his signature emphasis on "Love your neighbour as yourself," and the ways he expanded its philosophical and practical applications (beyond anything ever before conceived in history); along with his many and even ubiquitous practical Mitzvah campaigns—all inspired Eli and shaped his Hasidic approach to life and his work with others. As a naturally sunny person, the Rebbe's focus on the centrality of joy was something Eli connected with and integrated easily. He brought that signature joy to all he did and how he lived.

A PASSIONATE EDUCATOR

Small wonder that over time, without being preachy, condescending, or sanctimonious, he managed to turn every encounter into a meaningful, hands-on learning experience. He saw teaching moments as opportunities for joy. That's why when he first met Nikki Goldstein's family in the hospital, he naturally encouraged them to give *tzedakah*—so that a teaching moment became a way to fuse the spiritual with the temporal and connect with God.

It was crystal clear to Eli that you do not change the world with slogans. You change it with actions. Every mitzvah trains a conscience, builds a culture, and slowly creates a strong, healthy, vibrant community with a powerful moral immune system. That is why when he'd place a coin into a charity box, he'd treat it as something cosmic. That is why he could light a menorah in public and treat it as a Divine connection between heaven and earth: *God is here. Light is here. Do not surrender the world to darkness.*

Seamlessly, without artifice but with a genuine love for humanity, he helped people heal, grow, and feel fulfilled by taking actionable, tangible steps to celebrate the presence of God in their lives.

THE IMPERATIVE TO NOTICE

Eli made it his business to notice the people who slipped through the cracks, those who went unseen by most. He brought light into places where people feel there is no light. He brought dignity to people who were treated like numbers. He brought joy to people who had forgotten that joy was still permitted.

In hospitals, in prisons, in the exhausting, unglamorous corridors where human beings might be frightened, lonely, ashamed, or lost, his was a soothing presence, an uplifting voice. He was constantly thinking up new ways to help others. Who hasn't been contacted for a while? Who might be embarrassed to ask? Who needs a phone call? Who needs a text message that says, in effect, "I see you, and you matter"?

He set up classes with what seemed like hundreds of people—individuals or groups, some in-person, most online, he made time for everyone. He was always connecting. Since his passing our family has heard from people from literally across the globe—some whom we know, most of whom we don't. "He reached out to me," they said. "He checked on me." "He remembered me." "He carried me through a dark time." The sheer number of lives he touched is far beyond what I believe an ordinary person can fit into just forty-one years.

Yet, despite all his passionate commitment and great achievements, he refused to become egotistical or full of himself. From the get-go it was never about him. It was about the other, about the mission, about alignment, about God.

In my own personal experience, right from the moment Eli married our oldest child, Chaya, he became our son just as much as Chaya is our daughter. And he became my right hand, in the fullest sense of the word.

My wife, Shternie, my children, my whole family and I, were lucky to have had Eli in our lives for eighteen years. Eli and my daughter Chaya have five beautiful children, Priva, Nossen, Roza, Ary, and the baby, Shimshi. We share our loss with the entire Schlanger family. Eli was born into a warm and vibrant Chabad family, the eighth of nine children, Boruch, Chani, Dena, Tzippy, Shmuli, Perele, Sorala, and Sheina of Rabbi Binyomin and Dobra Baila Schlanger. He was raised in a home filled with love, joy, and strong Jewish values, where Eli absorbed a deep connection to Hashem and the Rebbe's teachings.

It was from this ground that Eli blossomed into the man he became.

I depended on him in countless ways. He was not only tremendously resourceful but was a true partner in my work. In nearly every aspect of what I do—within the community, in my rabbinic responsibilities, and in my work both locally and internationally—Eli was right there with me, not in my shadow, but in a self-imposed distance from the limelight, from where he felt he could do the most good. His loyalty and dedication were simply unmatched.

Sometimes when a person belongs to the community in that kind of way, his or her family suffers. But Eli was, at the very same time, the best husband and the best father. He was present. He was devoted. He was thoughtful. He carried his children in his mind constantly. We have a tradition that teaches that a person should think at least half an hour a day about the education of his children. Eli thought about it throughout the day, every day. His children's physical, emotional, and spiritual welfare was always on his mind.

A NEW CHAPTER BEGINS

A couple of years ago, ignited by some of the Rebbe's teachings, Eli became excited about the Seven Noahide Laws. (As a yeshiva student in the 1980s I was personally present when the Rebbe delivered some of those analytical and scholarly—and yet entirely practical—speeches, and recall vividly the immense love and concern for all of humanity that permeated the Rebbe's teachings.) The Rebbe's clear and convincing prescription for healing society's ills by awakening the Noahide system had a profound effect on Eli, and his always-whirring brain started churning.

Eli came to understand—and to really, really care—that the Rebbe's mission to reawaken the Noahide Laws as a framework for modern life matters more now than perhaps ever before. He felt that we are all experiencing what happens when societies detach themselves from the stable moral anchor of God, the One to Whom we are all accountable.

We are watching the consequences of this deficit in real time, Eli said, in families, on streets, on campuses, in the media, and in parliaments. Moral confusion has been dressed up as moral sophistication. Right is called wrong. Wrong is called brave. Evil is presented as progress. Truth is a matter of taste. "Justice" is used as a political weapon. And everyone is walking around more lonely and upset that ever, the suicide rate among young people is at an all-time high—and this is decidedly *not* how things are meant to be!

"So what can be done?" Eli would ask. "Simple: Share the Noahide Laws!"

The Seven Noahide Laws are the moral architecture needed to keep civilization from collapsing into a jungle, to make it whole. Moreover, *these laws chart the path by which humanity can realise its true purpose and meaning.*

The Noahide Laws help us appreciate that morality is not—cannot be—invented by human beings in real time. Morality

has been revealed to us from Above—by Moses, at Sinai. It is objective. It is anchored in the One Who created human beings, created the world, and understands us better than we can possibly understand ourselves.

Flowing directly from there, the Noahide commandments build a culture where people do not look away. Where speech is carefully weighed. Where the weak are not crushed because they lack power. Where everyone is accountable, always, to the "Eye That Sees and the Ear That Hears." Where the law is not merely law, but a restraint on the animal soul, a protection of dignity, and an invitation to nurture and illuminate the innate Divine spark.

It is holiness applied to human life.

Eli was passionate about this new and awesome mission he'd discovered. He felt it in his bones, and he was driven. Suddenly, it seemed, out of nowhere, he was pressing full throttle ahead. He worked with local schools to kick off "Project Noah" to educate the city's youth about the Noahide Laws. Their very first event saw fifty high school kids elect to come learn about this universal code and its vision for a peaceful, cohesive world. And it kept growing from there. At one point Eli said he'd heard it being referred to as "the hottest thing in town."

But it all reached a crescendo after the highly providential encounter Nikki shared with us in the book. Many of the principles Eli had learned and lived had already converged for him in their first highly unlikely meeting. When he eventually discovered that Nikki was a respected writer, he saw it as the ultimate expression of Divine Providence, and something he must "harness" for maximum result. His passion had finally been matched with a commensurate channel. He said he wanted the effort to "go global."

Nikki says that Eli began talking about a book they might do together while she was still in the hospital. When she finally agreed (she said he was charmingly persistent), he relished the opportunity to convey the Rebbe's vision for the world—to share the wisdom of living by these values with as many people as possible, and especially to convey the Rebbe's message that every single human being can be an ambassador to disseminate these principles and values to his and her spheres of influence.

After some months of their work together, suddenly came the horrific cruelty and destruction on the first Chanukah eve. And suddenly the book felt more urgent than ever. And, propelled by real people like Nikki and Rena Rossner, who handed the baton to lighthouse and powerhouse Lisa Sharkey and her whole team, it took on a life of its own. It appears that every single individual involved gave selflessly of themselves way beyond the norm; each was personally invested to urgently get the message out to the world NOW—to bring healing, to bring hope, to bring light, to bring joy.

And now suddenly . . . here it is, a reality: You are holding the volume in your hands!

As you probably well know by now, this volume is not a philosophy project. It is not just another "nice idea." It is not a cultural artifact for a museum shelf. It is, in fact, a book of inspiration and insight and, in a very real and tangible way, it is also an extension of the very life of Rabbi Eli Schlanger.

And Eli saw the book not just as an educational tool, but as a way to inspire, to bring light to the world, and to guide society toward purpose, integrity, and joy. The idea that the principles he cherished—justice, kindness, devotion to God—could inspire others to act and make the world better filled him with energy and hope.

Because the point of all of this is that God is real, morality is real, and we are each personally accountable.

Eli lived that accountability with love.

And that's what he hoped to convey, together with Nikki, to you.

WHAT NOW?

When tragedy strikes, people want to do something—almost anything. And then, with time, the feeling dissipates. If Eli was running the show, he would not allow that. He would immediately turn pain into action. He would see a wound and insist that it become a channel, a catalyst for light.

That is the work that is now placed on our collective shoulders.

So I turn to you, dear reader, whatever your background and wherever you may be, and I say this:

If you want to honour Eli, please do not only admire him. Emulate him.

Take the Noahide Laws seriously. Treat them not as ancient trivia but as a moral road map. Refuse to live in a world where chaos, upheaval, and strife are normal. Build something far, far better and lasting. Watch everything around you transform—your home, your workplace, your community.

Start by choosing one concrete act, one mitzvah, to create light.

Give charity. Not as philanthropy, but as righteousness (*tzedakah*)—an alignment with Divine justice. As an appreciation that God entrusted us with His resources and trusts us to make the right choices to distribute them on His behalf to those in need.

Take a moment to think about God. Live honestly. Love faithfully. Act compassionately. Look for opportunities to speak positively to family members and colleagues. Build justice. Be accountable to God.

If you're Jewish, please also participate and grow in those unique Torah commandments for the Jewish people. Putting on tefillin and lighting Shabbat candles are all-time favourites to start your journey.

And while on the topic of mitzvahs . . . : *On behalf of my entire family, I'd like to express our deepest and most heartfelt gratitude to Nikki Goldstein. She truly brought Eli's passionate wish to life—his profound desire to share these ideas, ensure they're understood, and carry them forward. What had long lived as hope and intention became reality through her. But even more remarkable than what she accomplished was how she did it: With unwavering dedication, genuine care, and a love that reflected not only her affection for Eli, but also her deep respect for everything he stood for. This work exists because of her belief, her generosity of spirit, and the extraordinary love she poured into making it happen.*

ᘓ

Before closing, it might be worthwhile to point out here that as a loyal Chabad emissary, Eli did not want Jews to live reactively but proactively.

He also believed—quietly but fiercely—that Jewish survival and human decency are not separate projects. A society cannot be "advanced" if it cannot distinguish between justice and cruelty, between freedom and chaos, between compassion and indulgence.

In this vein, it is my painful but awesome responsibility to record that Rabbi Eli Schlanger, my son-in-law, was tragically not alone, but was one of fifteen people who were killed on that fateful day as they prepared to usher in Chanukah on Bondi Beach.

Let us say their names: Yaakov Levitan. Reuven Morrison. Alex Kleytman. Tibor Weitzen. Edith Brutman. Boris Tetleroyd. Boris and Sofia Gurman. Dan Elkayam. Ten-year-old Matilda Bee Britvan. Marika Pogany. Peter Meagher. Adam Smyth. Tania Tretiak. And Eli Schlanger.

Each of these special people sanctified God's name. Each of their lives shines, bright as a beacon, illuminating the path before us. They will never be forgotten. . . . But memory alone is not enough. Nor are words alone enough either. Instead, we are called upon to ensure they will live forever.

And so, I close with a fervent prayer: that the world will imminently reach the fullness for which it was created—that history's long labour births an era of clarity, harmony, and abiding peace. For this is the ultimate aim toward which every page of this book has quietly pointed: that the hidden purpose within all our striving be revealed, and that humanity together witness the flowering of a redeemed and perfected world.

Yehoram Ulman
Bondi, Australia
7 Adar, 5786 * February 24, 2026

Acknowledgements

The first person I have to thank is Rabbi Eli Schlanger, who brought his heart and soul to our conversations. I will miss him for the rest of my days. I would also like to thank his beautiful family, Chaya Schlanger and their five children, Eli's mother and father-in-law, Shternie and Rabbi Yehoram Ulman. I can't thank Rabbi Ulman enough for his contributions and commitment to this book. Rabbi Ulman brought his powerful intellect, wisdom, and generosity to the book in ways I could never have imagined. I want to thank Deborah Harris, George Eltman, and everyone at the Deborah Harris Agency. I owe a massive debt of gratitude to Rena Rossner, my incredible agent, who understood from the first second she saw the manuscript how important Eli's words were to the world, and the incomparable Lisa Sharkey and her amazing team at HarperCollins, including Maddie Pillari and Lexi von Zedlitz, who believed in this project from the start and worked tirelessly to bring this book to a big audience. Lisa was grieving the loss of her beloved husband during this period—her Herculean strength inspired me every step of the way. I'd also like to thank Brigitta Doyle, Jim Demetriou, Sophie Ambrose, Nicola Woods and the amazing team from HarperCollins Sydney, who have been wonderful supporters and sensitive editors, making this process a joy. Big thanks to Joel Simons and Isabel Prodger, who put wings on the back of this book for the UK. A special thanks to Evie Summers, who worked closely with Eli for many years and who held my hand and gave endless words of support. Finally, I must thank my friends and family, who have been amazing cheerleaders and pillars of strength: my sublime husband, Rowan Jacob; my beautiful, clever daughter, Liberty Jacob; my mother, Sue Goldstein; my sister, Georgie, and my brother, Andrew, and their children. I would also like to thank Brook Turner, John Ireland, Katrina Strickland, and Hugh Lamberton for sharing that fateful day on December 14 with Rowan and me, and for being such wonderful friends and an integral part of this story. My deepest thanks to Lou Johnson and Adam Simpson and Anna Spies for jumping in with sage advice at just the right time. And to my incredible, devoted friends Stephanie and Mark Williamson, Sarah Turnbull, Fred Verniere, Caroline Casey-Brown, and Michelle Le Forrest, who all played a role in bringing this book to life. I thank you all for your generosity and love.

There are three people I must thank, because without them, I wouldn't be here. My sincerest gratitude and thanks for many years of the finest and most devoted care to Professor Marshall Plit, Professor Laila Girgis and Professor Eugene Kotlyar, my "Holy Trinity" from St Vincent's Hospital, Sydney.

As is the case with any big project, there were many unseen hands that worked to bring this book to light. It would not have been possible without the tireless, deft, loving, and Godly hands of Rabbi Zalman Shmotkin. He undertook this project with such a big heart and a big mission. Many threads needed to come together, and he was the weaver. Rabbi Shmotkin was the religious expert assigned to the task, and he often worked through the night to ensure the book's integrity and correctness. Rabbi Ulman, the Schlanger family, and I all owe him a huge debt of gratitude. This wasn't an ordinary project, and it was my privilege to work with such a brilliant, kind, and devoted man. We will be friends for life.

Other wonderful rabbis contributed their time, love, and devotion to this book. Thank you to Rabbi Freeman for his generous support and beautiful work with the Epigraph and thanks to Rabbi Motti Seligson for his dedicated and inspired contribution to this work. My deepest thanks go to Rabbi Eli Rubin and Rabbi Meir Simcha Kogan for their contributions. Our thanks to Rabbi Heschel Greenberg for his thoughtful input. The book is better for their collective passion for wisdom and for sharing Eli's message with the world.

For more information about the timeless teachings shared in this book, please visit Chabad.org/ConversationsBook

❧

Rabbi Eli Schlanger was the eighth of nine children of Rabbi Binyomin and Dobra Baila Schlanger. He was raised in a home filled with love, joy, and strong Jewish values.

This foundation gave Eli the clarity and courage to lead his community at the Chabad of Bondi, where he spread light, warmth, and inspiration with the support of his precious wife and children, family, and friends.

With deep gratitude and love to our parents, who dedicated their lives to showing us what it truly means to care for every person around us, no matter their background.

—Eli's siblings

Dear Tatty,

Being raised by you has been the greatest gift of my life. The way you treated every person with such love and respect, while devoting everything to our family, set the standard for the kind of person I strive to be.

I will carry everything you've taught me for the rest of my life and will be forever grateful that I am your daughter.

Thank you, Ta.

—Priva Shlanger, on behalf of all Eli's children:
Nossen, Roza, Ary, and Shimshi

ဏ

I am deeply grateful to my father for taking on this work and helping fulfil Eli's vision.

To Nikki, whose belief in Eli's words helped bring them to light.

To my parents, my family, and Eli's family, thank you for your constant love and unwavering support.

To my beautiful children—you are our greatest blessing and our most meaningful legacy.

And to my dear husband, I miss you every day.

—Chaya Shlanger

Glossary

Adonai—My Lord; a spoken liturgical substitute for the Divine Name.

Ahavat Yisrael—love of Israel/love of one's fellow Jew; a classic Jewish ethical ideal: active love and solidarity with other Jews.

Alter Rebbe—"the first rebbe," commonly referring to Rabbi Schneur Zalman of Liadi, founder of Chabad and author of the Tanya.

Ani l'dodi v'dodi li—I am my beloved's and my beloved is mine. (Song of Songs 6:3)

Av HaRachamim—Father of Mercy; a classic Jewish title for God (also the name of a memorial prayer in Jewish liturgy).

Avodah Zarah—strange/foreign worship; a rabbinic term for idolatry. Talmudic tractate.

Ayin—nothingness; a Kabbalistic term pointing to the hidden Divine "nothing" from which all being flows. Kabbalistic literature uses the language of *ayin/yesh* ("nothing/something") to describe emanation and Divine concealment.

Baal—master/lord, also the name/title of a Canaanite deity, a prominent ancient idol-cult.

Ba'al HaNess—Master of the Miracle; an honorific title meaning one who is associated with miracles (in memory, merit, or tradition). It signals not "magic" but a Jewish idiom of merit/prayer/moral repair.

Bar mitzvah/Bat mitzvah—son of the commandment; coming of age into Jewish responsibility (traditionally at the age of thirteen for boys and twelve for girls).

Baruch Atah Adonai—Blessed are You, Lord; the opening formula of many Jewish blessings (berachot), said before or after certain experiences (food, mitzvot, wonders).

Baruch Hashem—Blessed is God / Blessed be The Name; a common phrase of gratitude and grounding, used in everyday speech (connected to avoiding casual use of the Divine Name).

Beinoni—an intermediate person. In the Tanya, the spiritual "middle" archetype: not a saint, not a villain; someone who experiences inner impulses but refuses to express them in thought/speech/action.

Beit Din / Batei Din—house of judgment; rabbinical court/s.

Beit HaMikdash—The Temple; the holy Temple in Jerusalem, the historical locus of korbanot (offerings) in biblical/Jewish tradition.

Berachah/Berachot—blessing/blessings. A spoken formal formula recited to acknowledge God as the Source of food, experiences, and mitzvot that frames an act (like eating) as conscious receiving rather than entitlement.

Birkas Hashem—blessing of the Name—a euphemistic rabbinic phrase used to avoid saying "curse God" directly; it reads as "blessing the Name," but refers to blasphemy/cursing.

Birkat Hamazon—blessing of the food (Grace After Meals). The formal after-blessing said after eating bread, rooted in the Torah's command to bless after being satisfied.

Birur HaNitzotzot—refining/elevating the sparks—a Kabbalistic idea that holy "sparks" are embedded in the material world and can be uplifted through mindful, ethical action.

Bnei Noach (also B'nei Noach)—the Children/Descendants of Noah; the traditional Jewish term for non-Jews understood as bound by the universal moral baseline of the Noahide Laws. Discussed in rabbinic literature in the context of universal ethics (e.g., *Talmud Sanhedrin* 56a–60a; Rambam, *Mishneh Torah, Melachim uMilchamot* chaps. 8–10).

Brit Milah—Ritual circumcision of a Jewish baby boy on the eighth day, marking entry into the covenant.

B'tzelem Elokim (Elohim)—in the image of God; the Torah idea that every human being bears a Divine imprint, giving each life inherent, nonnegotiable dignity.

Chabad (Chabad-Lubavitch)—a major Hasidic Jewish movement known for outreach (*schlichut*) and creating welcoming Jewish spaces worldwide, emphasising disciplined inner work, intellect shaping emotion, and bringing holiness into daily life.

Chafetz Chaim—desirer of life; the honorific name by which Rabbi Yisrael Meir ha-Kohen Kagan is widely known, drawn from the title of his major work on ethical speech.

Chalaf / Shechitah knife—the specialised knife used for shechitah; it must be perfectly smooth.

Chanukah (also Hanukkah)—the eight-day Jewish Festival of Lights, commemorating the re-dedication of the Temple in Jerusalem and the Maccabean victory.

Chesed—loving kindness, expansive giving, generosity, and care; a core Torah value and a central spiritual quality in Hasidic/Kabbalah teaching.

Chesed (as Divine "flow")—in mystical language, the Divine "mode" of expansive giving that creation receives.

Cheshbon HaNefesh—accounting of the soul; a practice of honest self-review: tracking motives, habits, and spiritual growth without self-loathing.

Dayan HaEmet—the True Judge/Judge of Truth; traditional Jewish phrasing used when confronting death and loss ("Baruch Dayan HaEmet").

Devorah/Deborah—Prophetess and judge who led Israel with wisdom and moral authority.

Din—justice/judgment; the principle of law as moral truth, not mere procedure.

Din Torah—Torah-based legal hearing: religious arbitration of disputes according to Jewish law.

Dinah—Jacob's daughter in Genesis; her story becomes a Torah case study in communal responsibility and moral failure; see Genesis 34.

Divine sparks/elevation—a Kabbalistic idea that physical things contain "sparks" of holiness that can be "raised" when used with intention and goodness.

Dor HaMabul—the Generation of the Flood: shorthand for the pre-flood society described as violent, corrupt, and spiritually unmoored.

Ein Sof—without end—the infinite, unknowable Divine essence beyond all limitation and naming; "God as infinity."

Elohim Acherim—other gods; biblical phrase describing idols or rival "powers" set up against the One God; Torah language used in the Ten Commandments and broader biblical polemic.

Eloka d'Meir, Aneina—literally, "God of Meir, answer me." A devotional formula, often paired with giving tzedakah (charity) as a merit-seeking act for finding a lost object; associated with Rabbi Meir Baal Ha-Nes.

Elul—the final month of the Jewish year (preceding Rosh Hashanah), traditionally devoted to reflection, return, and spiritual preparation.

Emet—truth; frequently invoked in Jewish ethics as something stable, enduring, and aligned with God.

Etrog—a citron fruit used ritually during Sukkot as one of the "Four Species." Rabbinic tradition identifies the "beautiful fruit" with the etrog.

Ever min ha-chai—a flesh from a living animal. The Fourth Noahide Law: the prohibition on eating flesh taken from an animal while it is still alive.

Gelulim—a term of contempt for idols; a derogatory biblical word for idols.

Genesis (Hebrew, Bereishit)—the first book of the Torah; the origin story of humanity.

Gilgulim—reincarnations/cycles; an esoteric Kabbalistic teaching about the soul's journey through multiple lives or "cycles."

Halachah (Halahkah)—Jewish law, literally "the way/the path." The body of Jewish legal tradition governing ritual, ethics, and daily life, drawn from the Torah and expanded through rabbinic interpretation.

Halbanat Panim—whitening the face, public humiliation; a serious ethical wrong described by the sages as akin to "spilling blood," because it drains someone's dignity in public.

Hamas—a Torah word in Genesis 6:11 often translated as "violence." In classical Jewish interpretation it can carry the sense of robbery, predatory taking, or corrupt social exploitation, the kind of "everyday stealing" that rots a society from the inside.

HaMotzi—Who brings forth; the special blessing over bread: *HaMotzi lechem min ha'aretz* ("Who brings forth bread from the earth").

Hashem—literally "the Name"; a reverent way of referring to God without pronouncing the Divine Name. Rooted in biblical reverence for God's Name.

Hasidic/Chassidic (Chasidut)—a Jewish spiritual movement (eighteenth century onward) emphasising joy, devotion, mysticism, and community life.

Hechsher—Kosher certification, a certification mark showing that a product/establishment meets kashrut standards under a supervising authority.

Hitbonenut—contemplative meditation/reflection, a Chabad/Hasidic method of focused contemplation designed to internalise an idea until it reshapes feeling and behaviour. Central in Chabad practice and the Tanya's method of mind-led devotion.

Kabbalah—received tradition; the Jewish mystical tradition exploring the inner dimension of Torah: Divine unity, creation, spiritual psychology, and the structure of reality. Classical texts include the *Zohar* (medieval) and later systems (e.g., Safed/Lurianic Kabbalah).

Kapparah—atonement/expiation; a classic religious register word for spiritual "covering" or cleansing, often used colloquially to frame a loss as a form of atonement ("better this than something bigger").

Karov—near/close; the root notion behind *korban*: intimacy, approach, nearness.

Kedoshim Tihiyu—You shall be holy; a Torah command framing holiness as a lived standard, not a mood; often cited as an ethical demand under pressure.

Kedushah—Holiness; literally "set apart," i.e., protected by boundaries.

Kiddush Hashem—Sanctifying the Name; making God's presence credible in the world through integrity and conduct.

Kippah (also yarmulke)—skullcap worn as a sign of reverence and awareness of God. A widespread Jewish practice.

Klipah (pl., klipot)—shell/husk; a Kabbalistic term for spiritual "coverings" that conceal Divine light.

Korban—offering/sacrifice, Temple offering; the word is tied to karov ("closeness/near"). Many teachings stress that its deeper meaning is *drawing near* to God.

Kosher/Kashrut—*Kosher* means "fit/proper"; *kashrut* refers to the system of Jewish dietary law governing permitted foods and their preparation (including separate utensils, kitchens, and various handling rules).

Kotzer Ruach—shortness of spirit/breath; a phrase associated with constricted spirit, despair, or inner narrowness, used here as "short breath" that fuels anger.

Lashon (also Leshon)—language/tongue.

Lashon Hakodesh—the holy tongue; a traditional term for Hebrew (and, in some contexts, Jewish sacred speech).

Lashon Hara—evil speech; gossip, slander, or harmful speech, even if technically "true." Treated as spiritually and socially destructive. Extensive rabbinic and later ethical literature (classically systematised by the *Chafetz Chaim* in modern times).

L'chaim (also l'ḥayim)—to life; traditional Jewish toast.

Leshon sagi nahor—the idiom/language of sagi nahor; a later label for euphemistic or "opposite" language: saying the reverse to soften harshness or avoid shame.

Leviticus (Hebrew, Vayikra)—the Hebrew name for the Book of Leviticus ("And He called").

Lishmah—for its own sake; doing a deed for God/truth itself, not ego, status, or reward.

Lubavitcher Rebbe, The (Rabbi Menachem Mendel Schneerson, 1902–1994)—the seventh leader of Chabad-Lubavitch; renowned for teachings that translate deep mysticism into lived daily practice.

Lulav—a palm frond (bundled with myrtle and willow) used with the *etrog* on Sukkot as part of the "Four Species."

Magen David—Shield of David; the six-pointed Jewish star symbol widely associated with Jewish identity and community.

Maimonides (Rambam)—Rabbi Moshe ben Maimon (twelfth century), towering Jewish legal philosopher and codifier; "Rambam" is the standard Hebrew acronym. *Mishneh Torah* is his central code.

Makkot (Tractate Makkot)—a tractate of the *Babylonian Talmud* dealing with legal penalties (including lashes), false witnesses, and broader ethical teachings.

Matzah—unleavened bread eaten on Passover; symbol of haste, humility, and liberation.

Mazal tov—literally "good fortune"; the standard Hebrew/Yiddish phrase meaning "congratulations."

Menorah (Chanukiah/Hanukkiah)—a seven-branched lampstand. (For Chanukah specifically, a nine-branched *chanukiah*, eight lights plus a helper candle, is used.) The Temple menorah appears in Exodus 25; the Chanukah lighting practice is discussed in rabbinic sources (e.g., *Talmud Shabbat* 21b).

Mesillat Yesharim—Path of the Just; a classic Mussar work by Rabbi Moshe Chaim Luzzatto outlining a "ladder" of spiritual and ethical refinement; eighteenth-century.

Messiah (Hebrew, Mashiach)—the anointed one; in Jewish thought, the future era of redemption and the healing of the world.

Met—dead/death.

Midat Ha-din—"The attribute of justice": strict, exact judgment where actions have real consequences.

Midat Ha-rachamim—"The attribute of mercy/compassion": judgment tempered by kindness and deep understanding of context.

Mishlei (Proverbs)—the biblical Book of Proverbs.

Mishnah—the foundational compilation of the Oral Torah and early rabbinic law, redacted around the early third century CE; basis for later Talmudic discussion.

Mitzvah (pl., mitzvot)—commandment; also used colloquially for a good deed done in service of God and others. Sacred obligations/practices that shape daily life.

Modeh Ani—I thank You; a short morning gratitude prayer said upon waking, thanking God for the return of one's soul. A widely adopted Jewish morning practice.

Mussar—ethical instruction/discipline; the Jewish tradition of ethical self-development in character, habits, restraint, and refinement. Rooted in biblical wisdom and rabbinic ethics, later systematised (notably in the nineteenth-century Mussar movement).

Nefesh—often translated "soul," but in many Jewish/Kabbalistic contexts it means life-force, vitality, instinctual energy—the animating layer.

Nefesh Elokit—Divine soul; in Hasidic/Kabbalistic psychology, the aspect of the self drawn toward God, meaning, and spiritual purpose. The "Godly soul," God-consciousness, moral elevation.

Nefesh HaBehemit—animal/animalistic soul; in Hasidic/Kabbalistic psychology, the life-force tied to instinct, appetite, comfort, and self-preservation. The appetite-driven, comfort-seeking, survival layer.

Nefesh ha'chiyunit—living vitality; a related term meaning animating life-energy.

Neshamah—soul/breath; a higher "soul" term often used for the spiritual life-force God places within a person.

Neshimah—the Hebrew word for breath, linked in teaching to *neshamah* (soul); used in homiletic/mystical association with soul-life and inner vitality.

Niddah (31a)—a "daf"/page in Tractate Niddah (Talmud) discussing family life, the body, and human formation.

Nitzotz—spark; Divine vitality present within creation, used to describe the spiritual work of elevating the material world through conscious action.

Noahide Laws—seven foundational moral laws in Jewish tradition considered binding on all humanity.

Oneg Shabbat—Shabbat delight/enjoyment; the idea that Shabbat is meant to be enjoyed, through food, rest, song, and intimacy, within holiness.

Oral Torah (Hebrew, Torah Shebe'al Peh)—the interpretive rabbinic tradition transmitted orally and later recorded (Mishnah, Talmud), alongside the Written Torah.

Passover (Hebrew, Pesach)—the festival commemorating the Exodus from Egypt.

Pe'ah—corner (of the field); the commandment to leave the field's edges unharvested for the poor to glean.

Pikuach Nefesh—saving a life; the principle that preserving human life overrides almost all other commandments.

Pirkei Avot—Ethics of the Fathers; also a tractate of the Mishnah focused on ethical teachings, character, and wise speech.

Pogrom—violent anti-Jewish attacks, especially associated with Eastern Europe; a key Jewish historical term.

Rabbi—my teacher/master; a Jewish religious leader and teacher, trained in Jewish law and learning.

Rabbi Akiva—one of the most influential early rabbinic sages (Tanna), central to halachic method and Jewish tradition; Mishnah/Talmudic canon.

Rabbi Elazar ben Azariah—a prominent early rabbinic sage (Tanna) quoted in Mishnah/Talmudic discussions.

Rabbi Meir Baal Ha-Nes—Rabbi Meir, Master of the Miracle; a famous Tanna (early rabbinic sage) around whom later Jewish folk-piety developed practices for tzedakah (charity) and prayer in moments of need—especially when something is lost.

Rabbi Sheshet—a Talmudic sage (Amora) associated in tradition with physical blindness and exceptional learning; connected to the expression *sagi nahor*. Appears throughout the *Babylonian Talmud*.

Rabbi Tarfon—an early rabbinic sage (Tanna), known for sharp legal reasoning.

Rashi—Rabbi Shlomo Yitzchaki (1040–1105); the foundational medieval Torah commentator whose *p'shat* (plain-sense) glosses became the "default companion" to many central Jewish texts.

Rodef—pursuer; a person actively pursuing someone to kill them (or commit certain grave harms); Jewish law requires stopping them, even with lethal force if no alternative exists.

Sagi nahor—much light / abundant in light; a Talmudic euphemism commonly associated with referring to a blind person (an inversion: calling blindness "great light"). Aramaic euphemistic style in rabbinic discourse; later writers generalise it as "saying the opposite" with gentleness.

Sanhedrin—the name of the ancient Jewish high court, also a Talmudic tractate dealing with courts, law, justice, and related ethical categories (including discussion of the Noahide Laws).

Shalom—peace/wholeness; not just the absence of conflict, but harmony and repair.

Shechitah—ritual slaughter; the halachic method of slaughtering permitted animals for meat, requiring a trained slaughterer, an exceptionally smooth, sharp knife, and a swift cut, with the aim of ensuring death occurs as quickly as possible and without unnecessary suffering.

Shehakol Nihyeh Bidvaro—that everything came to be by His word; a standard blessing formula said over many foods/drinks (including water) that don't have a more specific blessing category.

Sheker—falsehood/lie.

Shekhinah—the Divine Presence; God's "nearness" within human space and relationships.
Shema—Hear (often "Shema Yisrael/Hear O Israel"); the central Jewish declaration of God's oneness, recited daily; a core prayer-text affirming monotheism and covenantal identity.
Shemirat HaLashon—guarding the tongue; a discipline of ethical speech: learning the laws and building habits that prevent harm through words. Built from rabbinic law and popularised widely through the Chafetz Chaim's teachings.
Sheva Mitzvot Bnei Noach—Seven Commandments of the Children of Noah; the Hebrew name for the Seven Noahide Laws, Judaism's traditional universal ethical baseline for all humanity.
Shloshah Asar Ikkarim—the "Thirteen Principles of Faith," famously systematised as core Jewish beliefs.
Shloshah shutafin ba'adam—There are three partners in a human being.
Shmita—Sabbatical year (every seventh year) when the land rests and certain debts are released.
Shmuel/Samuel—Prophet and judge who guided Israel during a critical transition in leadership.
Shoah—catastrophe; the Hebrew term commonly used for the Holocaust.
Shochet—ritual slaughterer; a trained, observant specialist authorised under Halachah to perform shechitah (ritual slaughter). Traditionally expected to be learned and careful, treating the act as a sacred responsibility.
Shofar—a ram's horn sounded in Jewish ritual, especially associated with Rosh Hashanah and Yom Kippur, and with awakening the heart.
Shoftim v'Shotrim—judges and officers; the paired idea of moral guidance (judges) and enforcement (officers).
Shotrim—officers/enforcers; those tasked with upholding the court's authority and preventing overreach.
Siddur—order; the Jewish prayer book, organised according to the daily/weekly liturgy.
Simcha—joy; also used to mean a joyful life event (wedding, bar mitzvah, birth, etc.).
Song of Songs (Hebrew, Shir HaShirim)—a biblical love poem traditionally read as both human romance and a metaphor for the love between God and Israel.
Sotah 17a—a "daf"/page in Tractate Sotah (Talmud) discussing marriage and spiritual merit.
Sukkah—a temporary hut used during the Sukkot holiday, recalling wilderness fragility and teaching gratitude and impermanence.
Sukkot—the Jewish Festival of Booths, a pilgrimage festival centred on gratitude, harvest, and the experience of sheltering with God.
Tanya—foundational text of Chabad Hasidism by Rabbi Schneur Zalman of Liadi; maps the inner struggle between animal and Divine drives and offers a practical spiritual psychology (late eighteenth, early nineteenth century).

Taryag Mitzvot—the traditional count of 613 commandments in the Torah incumbent upon Jews as part of the Sinai covenant.

Tefillah—prayer; both structured liturgy and inner devotion; the daily practice of turning the mind and heart toward God.

Tefillin—black leather boxes and straps containing Torah passages, worn (traditionally by Jewish men) during weekday morning prayer.

Tehillim—Psalms; prayers/poems of praise, protest, longing, and trust, used for daily devotion and in times of need. The Hebrew name for the Book of Psalms.

Teshuvah—return; often translated as repentance, but literally "return": returning to God, to truth, to the uncorrupted self.

Tetragrammaton (YHWH/יהוה)—the four-letter Divine Name in the Hebrew Bible, treated as uniquely sacred and not pronounced casually.

Tikkun—repair/rectification; the Kabbalistic idea of spiritual repair: transforming damage into restoration through conscious action, speech, and intention.

Tohar HaNeshek—purity of arms; the idea that the use of force must be restrained and morally governed; often invoked as an ethical ideal in warfare.

Torah—literally "instruction/teaching"; the foundational revealed text of Judaism (commonly referring to the Five Books of Moses, and more broadly the Jewish covenantal tradition).

Tza'ar ba'alei chayim—the suffering of living creatures; the Jewish legal-ethical principle that prohibits causing unnecessary suffering to animals.

Tzedakah—often translated as "charity," but more precisely "justice/righteous giving."

Tzimtzum—contraction; Kabbalistic teaching that God "contracts" or conceals Infinite Light to make space for creation's finitude and freedom.

World to Come (Hebrew, Olam HaBa)—the "world beyond"; a term for the afterlife/ultimate spiritual reality in rabbinic Judaism; often used as the arena of enduring consequence.

Yetzer Hara—evil inclination; the human impulse toward ego, self-gratification, and unrefined desire; not "a demon," but a moral/spiritual challenge to be directed.

Yetzer Tov—good inclination; the human impulse toward goodness, conscience, responsibility, and spiritual integrity.

Yisrael (Israel)—the name of Jacob and, by extension, the Jewish people; also "Israel" as a collective address in prayer ("Hear, O Israel").

Yom Kippur—Day of Atonement; the holiest day in the Jewish year, marked by a twenty-five-hour fast, prayer, repentance, and communal reflection.

Yovel—Jubilee year (the fiftieth year), associated with release and the return of ancestral land holdings.

Zohar—splendour/radiance; the foundational work of Kabbalah (written largely in Aramaic), central to later Jewish mysticism.

About the Authors

Rabbi Eli Schlanger was the assistant rabbi at Chabad Bondi, a role he had held for eighteen years. He was also a Chaplain for New South Wales Corrective Services and a chaplain at St. Vincent's Hospital, Darlinghurst, in Sydney. He was the rabbi for Community Engagement at Friends of Refugees of Eastern Europe for eighteen years. He was educated at the Central Lubavitch Yeshiva Tomchei Tmimim and the Lubavitch Yeshiva, Brunoy, France. Rabbi Schlanger oversaw the development and building of the Bondi Chabad. He was an active community rabbi and was passionate about outreach. He was the founder of Project Noah, an educational initiative that brings the timeless values of the Seven Noahide Laws to young people with engaging, interactive programs. He is survived by his wife, Chaya, and their five children.

Nikki Goldstein is an internationally recognised bestselling author of sixteen books—including *GirlForce*, a teen girl self-empowerment series that was converted into a brand of yoga wear, cosmetics, stationery, and music sold exclusively by Target—and an award-winning copywriter and journalist. She began her career at *Vogue* and held senior editorial positions at *Elle* and *Marie Claire*. When she's not working feverishly on her fledgling publishing business Go2Guru, Nikki attends to her two needy dachshunds, Archie and Sunny, and does yoga on her deck in Sydney.